W9-COZ-119

The Nubian Wedding Book

Words and Rituals to Celebrate and Plan an African~American Wedding

▼

Crown Publishers, Inc.
New York

The Nubian Wedding Book

by Ingrid Sturgis

Grateful acknowledgment is made to the following for permission to reprint previously published material:

Brown University Library: "A Golden Wedding" by Rev. T. Burleigh. Used by permission of the Brown University Library.

Howard University: Two letters from the Charles Drew papers at Moorland-Spingarn Research Center at Howard University.

Haki Madhubuti: "The Union of Two" by Haki Madhubuti. Reprinted by permission of the author.

The Crisis Publishing Co., Inc.: "So the Girl Marries" by W.E.B. Du Bois from *Crisis* magazine, the magazine of the National Association for the Advancement of Colored People. Reprinted by permission of the Crisis Publishing Co., Inc. The author wishes to thank the Crisis Publishing Co., Inc., the magazine of the National Association for the Advancement of Colored People, for authorizing the use of this work.

Thunder's Mouth Press: "A Modern Marriage" from *The Collected Stories of Chester Himes* by Chester Himes. Copyright © 1990 by Lesley Himes. Reprinted by permission of the publisher, Thunder's Mouth Press.

The University of Massachusetts Press: Two prayers from *Prayers for Dark People* by W.E.B. Du Bois, edited by Herbert Aptheker. Copyright © 1980 by the University of Massachusetts Press. Reprinted by permission.

▲

Grateful acknowledgment is made to the following for permission to reprint previously published photographs:

The New York Public Library and Joyce Hansen: Wedding Party (p. iii) and Wedding Service (p. 8), Austin Hansen photographer. Reprinted by permission of the Photographs and Prints Division, Schomburg Center for Research in Black Culture, Astor, Lenox and Tilden Foundations, Austin Hansen Collection and Joyce Hansen.

The Library of Congress: The Ebony Bridal (p. 22). Reproduced from the Collections of the Library of Congress.

Frank B. Lake: photo of Modestine and Edmund B. Lake (p. 26).

Corbis-Bettman: The wedding of Mr. and Mrs. Edward West and Mr. and Mrs. Oliver Sparks (p. 38) and wedding photo of a Haitian officer and his bride (p. 75). Reprinted by permission of UPI/Corbis-Bettman.

The Western Reserve Historical Society: Frank Spike and Margerie Hall, 1929 (p. 46); unidentified photo, p. 268 (p. 54); Herbert Butts, 1953 (p. 94); Sgt. Washington Haynesworth, 1945 (p. 122); Alex and Susie Johnson, ca. 1925 (p. 138); Charles Porter, 1946 (p. 162). Reprinted by permission of the Western Reserve Historical Society, Cleveland, Ohio.

The New York Public Library: Military Wedding (p. 68) and Wedding Postcard (p. 150). Reprinted by permission of the Photographs and Prints Division, Schomburg Center for Research in Black Culture, Astor, Lenox and Tilden Foundations.

Afro-American Historical and Cultural Museum: wedding photo, posed before monument (p. 180). Jack Franklin Collection, reprinted by permission of the Afro-American Historical and Cultural Museum.

Copyright © 1997 by Ingrid Sturgis

Published by Crown Publishers, Inc., 201 East 50th Street, New York, New York 10022. Member of the Crown Publishing Group.

Random House, Inc. New York, Toronto, London, Sydney, Auckland

http://www.randomhouse.com/

CROWN is a trademark of Crown Publishers, Inc.

Printed in the United States of America

Design by Lynne Amft

Library of Congress Cataloging-in-Publication Data is available upon request.

ISBN 0-517-70501-X

10 9 8 7 6 5 4 3 2 1

First Edition

To my mother, Ozia Sturgis,
and to the loving memory of my father, Jimmie Sturgis,
who always read everything I wrote

Contents

Acknowledgments

The Nubian Wedding Book is the result of a collective effort on the part of myself and many friends, acquaintances, and family. I especially want to thank my husband, Edwin B. Lake, who weathered many storms as I labored to bring this project to fruition. Thanks to my agent, Denise Stinson, who believed in me even before she knew me and who encouraged my early efforts. I want to thank my dear friend Yanick Rice Lamb, who listened to my ideas for this book for years and who was instrumental in sending this opportunity my way. I thank also my editor, Carol Taylor, who supported my efforts even as I worried and fretted over each step of the process.

I want to thank everyone who responded to my questions, and especially those who understood early on what I was trying to do even before I realized what an undertaking it would be. Thanks especially to Miriam Tarver, Melanie Eversley, Jared McCallister, Vanessa Williams Snyder, Michael Days and Angela Dodson, Connie Aitcheson, Judi Shimel, and Nicole Daniels, who unselfishly gave me essential assistance and lent undivided attention when I needed to talk.

Additional thanks to Crystal Wilkinson, who responded to my E-mail message and provided me with some remarkable sources. I thank my family members, particularly Colette Sturgis, Judy Bethel, Mildred Bethel, Loren Sturgis, and everyone who supported my efforts and provided me with suggestions, critical help, and encouragement. I thank Pastor Emmanuel Grantson, who is a fountain of knowledge and who was generous with his time as I struggled to make sense of my material.

And thanks to Ed Sims, Ann Grundy, Imani Hawkins, Linda Humes, Babalawo Ade Ifaleri Olayinka, Rev. Willie Wilson, Pam Hillsman, Deborah Lewis-Kearns, Thomas Snowden, Morris Jeff, Joyce Hansen, Leslie Willis, and Randall Pink.

The Nubian Wedding Book

Introduction

A wise African once said there are as many wedding customs as there are families. Although these customs serve the same essential purpose throughout the world, attending a wedding gives a guest an inside look at how two families merge their most cherished traditions.

Like a rich gumbo, *The Nubian Wedding Book* offers tasty tidbits of information about what sisters and brothers are doing to blend their cultural legacy into a wedding to remember. It is a compendium of writings and rituals that offers practical ideas and romantic touches to allow couples to create a family wedding, as well as a source to inspire culturally significant wedding ceremonies.

Within these pages is a bounty of information gleaned from historical records, wedding consultants, engaged and married couples, pastors, spiritual leaders, and other people involved in the culture of weddings. Each section explores a different component of love, mating, and marriage. There are dozens of suggestions for blending your heritage into a celebration that enriches and illuminates the customs that we cherish, including anecdotes from several couples on their personalized weddings, historical details about traditions from Africa, the Caribbean, and the United States, as well as expert opinions on incorporating family and friends into any ceremony.

The idea for *The Nubian Wedding Book* started about eight years ago when Edwin Lake and I got married. I went to several bookstores trying to find a book that would offer me ideas about celebrating my African-American heritage. No such book existed.

As a journalist who has written many articles and essays about black arts and culture, I realized that most of this information would not be easy to come by. Although there are far more books written by and for African Americans these days, as few as eight years ago many of the stories that I wrote about African Americans required firsthand interviews for a significant portion of the research. I knew I'd have to do a little digging.

But with the wedding plans, moving to a new apartment, and taking a new job that required several hours of travel a day, I had no time to dig. Yet my interest set me on a long journey as I began to read, research, and collect any item or idea I could find that sought to reclaim our wedding customs. This book is the end result of that journey, a compendium of interviews, wedding tips, recipes, and extraordinary stories of love, betrothal, and marriage.

There is still a wealth of information about mating and marriage rituals among people of African descent that has yet to be fully uncovered. This book is an effort to go back and reclaim our heritage. Contrary to popular opinion, our families do create and uphold traditions and cultural mores. But sometimes we neglect to protect and preserve those valuable commodities.

There is a hunger for more details about our African, Caribbean, and African-American heritages. But instead of rejecting an American model for a more African one, many want to blend their cultural makeup to take from each aspect what they feel is most important to them.

I want to add *The Nubian Wedding Book* to their resources. It is designed to give couples and their families a fuller understanding of how this rite of passage has been celebrated through the ages. It also strives to be a historical record, a spiritual guide, and a family heirloom for those who want to maintain a link with their cultural heritage.

Herein you'll find details about wedding rituals in the motherland, where an elaborate courting ritual is a common thread among many African countries. When a young man finds the woman he wants to marry, it requires a series of negotiations, often over several weeks. Once settled, the bride recedes into seclusion, being pampered and protected until, upon the day of her wedding, she emerges to join her husband.

These ancient marriage ceremonies have managed to adapt and change as Africans modernize. For example, in some West African families, elders no longer await the tell-tale signs of virginity with a rigorous examination of the bridal bed. Instead, the ritual has become a more ceremonial undertaking as couples now use drops of animal blood to satisfy custom.

Included are details from slave narratives regarding weddings of couples who were not permitted to marry legally but who pursued the quest for pageantry and ceremony by "jumping the broom" before they returned to their often separate dwellings. Some scholars feel this ritual has an African link and have discovered variations of the same in such places as Panama and Trinidad and Tobago.

Readers will find out about the wedding affair of couples like Delmar and Cheree Gillus, who created a ceremony and reception that blended aspects of their African and American heritage. She topped her white dress with an African crown and he topped his tuxedo with a *kufi*. And they entered into bridal registries that specialize in afrocentric gifts and furnishings.

During the wedding, they used the ancient ritual of libation to invoke the spirits of their forebears. Like their slave ancestors, they leaped over a broom into the land of matrimony. The guests then dined on a menu of African fare.

You will meet South Africans Siphokazi Koyana and Zola Pinda, who married in a civil ceremony in 1993 in Philadelphia. They defied Xhosa tradition when they met, got engaged, and married in a whirlwind courtship. But each time they return home they are compelled to carry out many of the traditions that their families have practiced for generations.

"We like to think we are westernized and far removed from it," says Sipho. "But each time we go back home we cannot be seen together without doing something to call on both families and until we have finished all the rituals."

There will be readings about love, including passionate love letters exchanged between nineteenth-century author and poet Paul Laurence Dunbar and his wife, Alice. There is a section on creating words of good wishes for the couple. There are descriptions of different types of libations, an ancient ceremonial rite that pays homage to ancestors, as well as toasts and other words of blessing to send a couple on their lifelong journey.

In the section on wedding vows and ceremonies are words adapted from actual ceremonies that brides and grooms can personalize and incorporate into their own affairs. Although the vows may be used verbatim, they serve mainly as a guide for couples to use to create their own special moments.

There is a ceremony in which the Nguzo Saba, seven important principles to live by —unity, self-determination, collective responsibility, cooperative economics, purpose, creativity, and faith—are incorporated into wedding vows.

There is a ceremony that makes use of Yoruba practices, such as the tasting of kola nuts, a source of strength; honey, to add sweetness; water, to freshen; or pepper, also to test a groom's strength.

In addition, selections of prose and poems about love and marriage may be used to complement wedding vows, or on wedding programs, invitations, and thank-you notes. There is also vital information about finding a wedding planner and clergy who can help you create a ceremony with meaning and purpose.

For those interested in Caribbean traditions, included is a recipe handed down from mother to daughter for the Caribbean black cake that many brides find an essential part of their reception festivities. Suggestions for menus to use at wedding showers are also provided. And last, there are descriptions of prewedding rituals such as the *queh-queh,* a

DELMAR AND CHERÉE GILLUS CREATED A CEREMONY THAT BLENDED ASPECTS OF THEIR AFRICAN AND AMERICAN HERITAGE.

ceremony of dance, drums, and songs that many brothers and sisters from Guyana revel in just before their wedding.

The book ends on a note of renewal as couples whose unions have longevity reveal the source of their marriages' strength and resilience.

You can then turn to the Resource Guide for a listing of goods and services geared toward the afrocentric wedding celebration.

Now, in the spirit of *Sankofa*—go back and fetch it.

Part 1

To Be Loved

Where God is, love is.

AL GREEN

The Road to Matrimony

Committing to Love

The quest for love is one of the strongest impulses of the human spirit. As children, we bask in the glow of love from our parents and family, the people who satisfy our needs. But as adults, we could spend a lifetime searching for a soul mate, someone we can trust, someone on whom we can depend, someone who gives us what we couldn't find in our family relationships. When we find that person, together we move toward a more permanent state—marriage. However, the road to matrimony involves risk. Lovers who dare to open their hearts are at risk of having them broken. But by taking that risk, they learn to trust. They learn to accept mistakes and believe in promises made. Lovers find that to give of themselves freely exposes them to the transforming power of love. With love, all things become possible. That we love passionately and with abandon has been recorded throughout time in love letters, poems, essays, narratives, and folklore. The quest for companionship and true love blossomed even during slavery when black men and women were often discouraged from engaging in loving relationships. During slavery, harsh slave masters mated men and women without regard to love or even compatibility. Such relationships were seldom secure because, as chattel, slaves could be sold at a moment's notice.

But even under such uncertain conditions, human desire flourished. An unidentified observation from the Fisk University slave narratives reveals that during the era of slavery and Reconstruction, dating concerns paralleled those of today.

"They courted as they do now. Only they wasn't fast like they are now. I never in all my born days went out at night by myself and stayed out like these young folks do now. When I went out I always had company."

Folklore also records that our antebellum ancestors developed their own unique style of courtship, filled with formality and eloquence. Then as now, the man was often expected to initiate conversation.

He might say: "My dear kin miss, has you any objection to me drawin my cher to your side and revolvin de wheel of my conversatin arund de axle of your understanding?"

She might reply: "I has no objection to a gentleman addressing me in a proper manner."

Another interested gentleman might have used this opening line: "Kin lady, is you a towel dat has been spun or a towel dat has been woven?"

To which a single woman might answer that she is spun. Put together by her parents, she is still available as a mate.

Or another would ask:

"I saw three ships on the sea, one full-rigged, one half-rigged, and one with no rigging at all. Which one are you?" The woman would answer appropriately: full-rigged for married, half-rigged for engaged, and no rigging, single.*

---

*From *A Treasury of Southern Folklore* by B. A. Botkin (New York: Random House, 1988).

Lucy Ann Dunn of North Carolina recalled her courtship with Jim Dunn, shortly after emancipation.

"It was in de little Baptist Church at Neuse where I first seed big black Jim Dunn and I fell in love with him den, I reckons. He said dat he loved me den too, but it was three Sundays before he asked to see me home.

"We walked dat mile home in front of my Mammy, and I was so happy dat I ain't thought it a half a mile home. We et corn bread and turnips for dinner and it was night before he went home. Mammy wouldn't let me walk with him to de gate. I knowed, so I just set dere on de porch and says good night.

"He come every Sunday for a year and finally he proposed. I had told Mammy dat I thought I ought to be allowed to walk to de gate with Jim and she said all right, iffen she was settin dere on de porch."*

Nineteenth-century romantic poet and author Paul Laurence Dunbar found his true love through her writings. Through extended correspondence, Dunbar's relationship with his future wife, Alice Ruth Moore, grew—at the same time as his celebrity. Dunbar claimed that Alice inspired his work, and he dedicated several poems to her.

A treasure trove of their passionate letters reveals their stormy affair. After several months of writing, Paul finally met Alice when she stole away to meet him before he left town for another appointment. They immediately became engaged. The time they spent apart only inflamed their love for each other. Their feelings were no less ardent during their short periods of reconciliation.

In one letter, Dunbar wrote, "I think of you and close my eyes with that sensuous slowness which one adopts when one is being kissed to the fainting point."

---

*Life under the "Peculiar Institution": Selections from the Slave Narrative Collection, Norman R. Yetman, ed. (New York: Holt, Rhinehart & Winston, 1970).

Moore responded, "You have played me an unfair trick, heart of mine; you have so completely woven yourself into the thread of my life until I cannot imagine an existence apart from you."

Dunbar's love for Alice was a transcendental, unearthly love without regard to daily issues. But daily issues did intrude. Alas, although their love for each other would last, their marriage would not.

But many passionate affairs stand the test of time. Olwen E. Gillman of the Bronx met her true love at the age of thirteen. Edwin was eighteen.

"I met a gentleman who was supposed to be a cousin of mine. He was like Adonis. I went to his mother's house with my mother to meet him. He was an accomplished tailor. He was a man."

Edwin felt the same way. From a respectable distance, they both watched as the other matured. Their families were vigilant. He kept a respectable distance and their families observed a protocol needed to protect Olwen. "He watched me as I continued to watch him. Everyone said I was the lotus in the pond that the frog was watching until I was ready to receive him."

Edwin began to pay visits to Olwen at her family's apartment house in the Bronx. He came Monday through Saturday evenings.

Then Edwin got the nerve to ask to take Olwen to the movies. It became a ritual.

"Every Saturday night, we went to the Apollo until I was twenty-two," Olwen said. "He gave me a birthstone ring. A topaz —a friendship ring until he could afford a diamond. I told him that he would have to ask my mother and father and write them a letter. It was in my mother's effects when she died."

In 1946, Edwin followed the custom common for people of Caribbean heritage—a young man would write a letter to the parents of his intended to ask for her hand in marriage. Olwen said the letter her future husband wrote to her parents was simple and direct: "Dear Mae and Felix: I would like to ask your permission to have your daughter in marriage. Respectfully, Edwin."

They spent five years building a friendship. "I knew I could handle him. I was twenty-three when we were married. Edwin was twenty-eight. He knew I was naive and young. I had had no dates. I was a fresh, young plum. I loved him so. It was unadulterated. It was pure. I forgave him each step. We were married for forty-nine years."

WITH A
RADIANT GLOW
ON HER FACE,
OLWEN DANCED
WITH HER
NEW HUSBAND,
EDWIN GILLMAN,
AT THEIR WED-
DING IN 1946.

Matrimonial Transformation

Throughout society, marriage is considered the final rite of passage on the road to adulthood. By publicly declaring their intent, a bridal couple signals the seriousness of their undertaking. The engagement is the period in which the bride and groom begin their transformation into husband and wife. It is marked with celebrations and festivities heralding their emergence into broader society. The engagement is also a dress rehearsal for the new status and responsibilities that the lovers will assume as husband and wife. Not only are the lovers sanctioned to spend more time with each other, they are encouraged to become acquainted with a wider milieu—their circle of family and friends who make up the community in which they will reside.

In the Caribbean and many African countries, it once was customary for the wedding announcement—banns—to be issued in church a few weeks before a wedding. Not only was it a formality to announce the approaching nuptials, the banns was a method to determine any previous claims on the betrothed couple. Read on three consecutive Sundays to give anyone with objections an opportunity to be heard, it helped deter misunderstandings by spurned lovers as well as fraudulent intentions by the bride or groom.

In that same spirit, announcements today are published in newspapers, usually as much as a year in advance. On a personal level, a couple might send notes to family members and friends to make the announcement. And today's bride and groom can even announce their engagement at cyberspace wedding sites on the Internet.

Starting in ancient Egypt, men have marked the occasion of their engagement by giving their betrothed a ring. Like a circle, considered a symbol of eternity in Egyptian hieroglyphics, the ring symbolized the eternal bond of marriage. A gold ring—a gift of value—customarily sealed the betrothal and helped bind the marital contract. Women wear it on the fourth finger of the left hand, since it was romantically thought that a vein from that finger ran straight to the heart.

The engagement's transitory period is marked by celebration and transformation in many African families. The elder members of the two families might share a smoke from a pipe to salute their new alliance. And the man's family seals the marriage agreement by taking such gifts as beer, cattle, kente cloth, and food to the bride's family. (If the marriage is not successful, these gifts must be returned.)

The World of the Swahili by John Middleton details the complex process leading to marriage. Before the wedding, the bride and groom receive counseling and advice from a community of elders. A trusted woman—an aunt or older sister—will become the guardian and teacher of the bride. She is charged with such duties as inviting and assisting with the guests, offering marital advice, tending to the bride's needs, and preparing cosmetic rituals for her wedding day. Similarly, a designated man oversees preparations for the groom.

Revered for their knowledge and wisdom, the elders are the counselors and advisers that married couples can turn to in times of dispute and trouble. These guardians make sure the families adhere to ancient customs, they oversee the exchange of bridal payments between the families, and they may mediate disputes between families.

Even today, counseling is considered one of the most important premarital preparations by nearly every spiritual adviser. Deciding to make monogamy a commitment after a life of singlehood may require adjustments that would benefit from professional and experienced insight. Every couple can benefit from spiritual, psychological, or emotional counseling, particularly those who have issues about divorce or parenting.

Some wedding planners say the couples they meet with are so involved in the wedding plans that they don't take time to get to know each other before the big day. Weddings often release so many emotional issues, not just for the bride and groom but for other family members as well, that counseling is essential to help the participants understand the emotional and physical changes that come with marriage.

Sessions with a counselor, elder, or spiritual adviser should cover various elements of a modern marriage. The issues may include the following.

CHILDREN

Will you practice birth control? Which method? How many children will you have? How long will you wait to have them? Will husband or wife stay home to raise the children? How have you agreed to handle raising them? How will you plan for day care? Do you have children from other relationships? How will they be integrated into your family life? Where will they live? How will the children be disciplined?

FOR THE COUPLE

Where will you live? Will you both work full-time? How often will you entertain guests? What are your expectations about marriage? What do you consider important elements of the man's role in marriage? What about the woman's role? How will you handle disagreements?

FINANCES

How will you handle major purchases such as a car or house? Who will take care of paying the monthly expenses? How much will you save each week? Will you buy a house or rent? How often will you shop for clothes? Do you think a prenuptial agreement is important?

RELIGION

What part will spirituality play in your marriage? If you have different faiths, how will you handle child rearing? Do you plan to tithe? Will you both attend a house of worship? Will you both get involved in church affairs?

FAMILY

What kind of relationship do you have with your parents? How will your relationship with them affect your marriage? What about your relationships with siblings, family members, friends? How will this affect your relationship with your spouse? Do you need time to be with your friends? How much? How will you handle friendships of the opposite sex?

SEX

How often do you think is reasonable to have sex? How important is intimacy to you? Are you open to new things sexually?

Embracing Custom and Creating Tradition

▼ ▼

Marriages Across the Motherland

In Togo and parts of Nigeria, the bride literally undergoes a transformation as she is fattened up for marriage, according to Florida wedding planner Olga Byll, who is originally from Togo. For fourteen days before the wedding, the bride will reside in a fattening room where her family tries to evoke her full feminine aura by making her as plump as possible to show how well they have cared for her. Her voluptuous figure and glowing skin signify both pure beauty and fertility—that she is full of life and full of fruit. The woman is fed, cleansed, and beautified and offered advice by the elder women in her family. Similarly in Lamu, an island off the coast of

THIS HARLEM COUPLE STOOD BENEATH THE HUPPAH AT THEIR JEWISH CEREMONY.

Nigeria, brides-to-be receive beauty treatments marking their new status as a married woman. Henna is used to draw designs on their hands and feet. An elder comes to help wash the bride's hair and to bathe her. She will be massaged with coconut oil to soften her skin and rubbed with oils of sandalwood and aloe to keep her smelling sweet. Outside her secluded chamber, her family and the groom's engage in a succession of feasts and celebrations to rejoice at the nuptials.

In Morocco, the engagement may last several months, during which time the man sends his fiancée gifts of jewelry, cloth, dresses, and perfume on important holidays. In other societies, the woman and man may undergo initiation rites, including circumcision,* sexual initiation, and other rituals, to prepare them for marriage.

The mothers-in-law of Ndebele women in southern Africa make the bride a *jocolo*—the five-paneled, exquisitely colorful, beaded goatskin apron that all married women wear on ceremonial occasions.

These engagement rituals help to strengthen the interdependence and cooperative spirit between the families of the betrothed. The giving of premarital gifts and services to each other's families helps to cement the marriage agreement.

Although many of these customs are tied to age-old concerns of collective survival, most still are practiced in villages and towns throughout Africa. Family elders continue to guard the rites and rituals to protect and uphold social order.

Though the rituals show signs of adapting to a modern era, they are considered outdated vestiges of a bygone era by many in a more assimilated younger generation who are discarding traditional forms of marriage, opting for a westernized version of matrimony. And some scholars say because of this, marriages in Africa are showing the same signs of stress and strain as marriages in the United States.

---

*Female circumcision has come under fire as African women mobilize to stop the practice. In one widely publicized incident, Fauziya Kassindja fled Togo and sought asylum in the United States rather than undergo the mutilation of her genitals in preparation for an arranged marriage. In severe cases, women are maimed and some die in the traditional ritual. In other instances it deadens sexual pleasure and may cause a lifetime of gynecological problems, including infertility.

Reestablishing Cultural Ties

Even as some Africans abandon their family customs, many African Americans in the United States are searching for ways to embrace them. Some historians say because of our legacy of slavery, we lack the inherited knowledge of our foreparents. And this lack of knowledge about our ancestry, combined with the destruction of family ties during three centuries of slavery, has made our family relationships more vulnerable.

Never have we been more aware of the frailties in our relationships than today, when some statistics note there are more African Americans remaining single than getting married. As reflected in society at large, African Americans are experiencing a high rate of divorce. Statistics reveal that more children are born out of wedlock than in a marriage. And many point with pessimism to the breakdown in family life as a precursor to a breakdown of society.

But despite the odds, most of us still optimistically seek companionship and family. Instead of eschewing rites and rituals as old-fashioned and meaningless, many African Americans are starting to reconnect to family and ethnic customs. Unlike the situation in Africa, African Americans are bound by no formalities to betrothal. Most people don't need their family's approval to meet and marry. But many who are seeking more meaningful relationships have come to mine the past to provide direction and add significance to their engagements.

Couples today are making an effort to establish rituals that bring more meaning and ceremony to their engagements and subsequent marriages. In addition to the usual whirl of showers and parties, they are opting for more personal and private statements that attest to their love and devotion for each other. Some become involved in formal couple-mentoring programs through their churches. Or as part of their wedding ceremony, some ask older couples who are close family friends to serve as elder advisers or counselors for the early years of their marriage. The counselors then agree to offer insight and guidance to both husband and wife during the trials and tribulations of marriage.

Some of these rituals may be based on African customs and are an opportunity for the families of the bride and groom to draw closer to the traditional communal nature of family, while others take their cues from religious or family rituals.

The Counsel of Elders

Daryl Perry and Theresa Parris-Perry of the Bronx sought the counsel of elders before their 1995 marriage, which came after a nearly seven-month courtship. They started with a reading and counseling by a Yoruba priest, Babalawo Ade Ifaleri Olayinka. Theresa, who had traveled to Ghana and Nigeria, said the consultation was important. "We knew it's not just us. It's bigger than us. We have commitments to other people. It was a family kind of wedding. I marry you and everything attached to you," said Theresa.

They talked with family, friends, and mentors at the National Black Theater in Harlem where both were volunteers. Daryl took the formal step of asking Theresa's stepfather for her hand in marriage. He talked with her stepfather and mother, who asked many questions about his ability to support and care for a wife.

What helped cement their relationship, they say, was a workshop they took at the National Black Theater. It helped give them a more spiritual focus and a better understanding of their black heritage. "It was just a feeling that this tied everything together spiritually," said Daryl. "I was ready to take the next step in our journey. I never had a relationship where we talked so much about reactions, moods. It was more of a spiritual relationship."

They decided to hold their wedding at the theater's African temple, a beautiful sanctuary filled with walls of hammered copper and brass and with sculptures and paintings, all created by African artists and artisans.

Some churches around the country, such as the Tenth Street Baptist Church in Washington, D.C., have mentoring programs to counsel couples on the road to marriage. Robert E. Black and his wife, Ella, have become advisers to many of the couples who come for premarital counseling in their marriage ministry. Married for over 30 years, they say they serve as mentors to honor the people who helped them through the rough places in their marriage. The couple act as role models and guides for the engaged, newlyweds, and those in long-term marriages. But particularly for engaged couples, they offer practical information about the rite of passage they are undergoing. "We create a relationship during that period. We set their minds to the times that there will be problems. It's a matter of how you deal with those problems. We let them know that the Bible has all the answers," Robert Black said.

Together with the Rev. A. Michael Durant, Ella and Robert Black offer counseling sessions with engaged couples to provide a sound spiritual base for their upcoming marriages.

Some couples use fasting as a shared experience during their engagement. Fasting has a spiritual foundation in many religions, including Islam, Christianity, Judaism, and Yoruba. In the Bible, Christ as well as his Disciples fasted and prayed to overcome adversity and heighten their religious experience. Many religions recommend fasting as a means to purify the body and bring spiritual healing. Couples who fast attest to its ability to elevate the religious significance of their engagement.

Carolyn White-Washington and William Earl Washington, of Maryland, decided to fast until sundown each day for a month before their wedding. They also read books together on relationships and went to counseling with their pastor, the Rev. Willie Wilson in Washington, D.C.

"Before we got married, we fasted and prayed that God would give us confirmation on our vows. We fasted for spiritual direction. We know in order to get a word from God you have to fast and pray. I wanted a real revelation. I wanted to make sure God had brought us together. We had a chance to commune as one. It was spiritual. It helped me grow a lot. This was totally different," Carolyn said.

Others opt for celibacy in the period before their marriage. Some ministers encourage it to honor what many call God's original intention.

Although Crystal Worsley and her husband, Paul Worsley, of Maryland, dated for five years, they decided to remain celibate for five months before their marriage. "This is something we are doing before God and we wanted to make these vows and do it correctly," said Crystal. "We had been thinking about it before we got engaged. Relationships are a lot more than the physical. We agreed. It helped us to focus on the wedding, spirituality, and counseling with the minister."

Others plan a variety of celebrations to get their families involved.

When Toni Booth-Comer and Vernon B. Comer of Columbus, Georgia, got engaged, they began a variety of public and private rituals to make their commitment special. They read the same books about relationships and marriage planning, and shared their thoughts so they could feel closer even though they lived in separate cities before their marriage. They also attended a weekend retreat for engaged couples for guidance and to gain support from others undergoing similar experiences.

Toni also relied on counseling to better understand marriage. "Because three months after dating, we got engaged. I wanted communication. I worked for a divorce lawyer. I wanted it to stay on the spiritual side," she said.

"All this stuff opened our eyes," she said. They were engaged for a year. "We found that we had a lot of the same ambitions the more we talked. We are both hotheaded. I had to stop. I had lived by myself. I had to learn to be considerate and give Vernon a chance to be concerned. I wasn't allowing him to care. I'm glad we went into these things. You don't go into marriage thinking about divorce."

They held a weekend family get-together to introduce each other to their families. "We worked it around the Christmas holiday. Everyone cooked a dish and brought it. I asked everyone to bring a universal gift for the adults and one gift for the kids. My family got to meet Vernon and he got to see my family in action." This gave Vernon a chance to talk to Toni's uncles and the cousins she grew up with.

Words on Love, Courtship, and Marriage

Writings about love best express the depth of our emotions during courtship. This chapter includes love letters by some of our most famous historical figures. Tender missives from the United States and Africa offer similar sentiments regarding love and relationships. Dr. Charles Drew, who discovered blood plasma, found his work and research interrupted with thoughts of his beloved Lenore Robbins. He wrote many letters to her as their relationship developed and after they married. (Drew died tragically in a car accident in 1950.)

NEWLY FROM ANTIGUA, MODESTINE AND EDMUND LAKE STRUCK A STATELY POSE IN THEIR ELEGANT WEDDING ATTIRE.

Lenore,

With a heart that's full with a new found joy my thoughts turn to you as the day closes and a sigh rises as an evening prayer to ask whatever gods there be to keep you safe for me. Since first seeing you I have moved through the days as in a dream, lost in reverie, awed by the speed with which the moving finger of fate has pointed out the way I should go. As the miles of countryside sped by on our return trip I sat silent and pondered on the power that lies in a smile to change the course of a life; the magic in the tilt of a head, the beauty of your carriage and the gentleness that struck so deeply.

Later when I become more coherent, I shall say perhaps many things but tonight this one thing alone seems to ring clearly, I love you.

Charlie

April 9, 1939

Darn it all Lenore,

I'm supposed to be here working but work is the farthest thing from my mind. I'm simply no good at it. It's terribly disturbing, disorganizing, inefficient, demoralizing, upsetting, frustrating, unaccountable, uncomfortable, enervating, understandable—delightful.

The sap has gone crazy, grins at himself, preens, struts, blushes, smiles, laughs, whistles, sings and then just sits in a daze. Got heartburn, palpitation, indigestion, anorexia, psychasthenia, euphoria and delusions of grandeur. Hallucinations by day and insomnia by night. Got misery and ecstasy, Dear Dr. Robbins what is my trouble? Only you can tell me. Please answer soon. I'm in bad shape.—Charlie*

---

*From The Charles Drew Papers, Moorland-Spingarn Research Center, Howard University.

Dunbar Letters

Already an acclaimed poet by 1895, Paul Dunbar was just twenty-three when he fell in love with Alice Moore through her published writings. She was twenty. They carried on a torrid love affair through the mail because Paul, who had become a literary sensation, traveled often to speaking engagements. They were married soon after the following letters were exchanged.*

Feb. 19, 1898

My Darling:

I am almost afraid to write to you today for fear that I shall say something that is not quite nice. Dear, your remark about wishing to be asleep in my arms has simply set me afire. I think of you and close my eyes with that sensuous slowness which one adopts when one is being kissed to the fainting point. My whole being palpitates with passion. My fingers tremble, they want to be running through your hair. My face rubs again your velvet cheek. I feel your breath on my lips. I feel your heart throbbing against mine. I hear your whisper—"My Paul," I reach for you—and you are not here.

Dear heart, it is best that we be not together much before we are married. It is a wise Providence that has sent me rushing these thousand miles away as soon as we became engaged and now keeps me chained in another city from you.

I am so glad, though, darling, that it is not a common, vulgar passion that I feel for you. There is something about it that positively uplifts me. Mind and soul are both blended in it, and if my eyes do grow brighter than their

---

*From "The Letters of Paul and Alice Dunbar" by Eugene Wesley Metcalf, Ph.D. dissertation, University of California, Irvine, 1973. In *Language and Literature, Modern* (Ann Arbor, Michigan: University Microfilms, A Xerox Co.).

wont. If the blood does speed hotter through my veins, if any breath does come in gasps, it is all for my own wife, and no illicit companionship could fill the want, the great yearning which I feel. Now hide your face and blush for the heat of Your Loving Husband.

Feb. 20, 1898

Dearest husband—I have just been doing what I suppose is a very foolish thing—leaning out of the window in my dressing gown and letting the rain beat on my head. It ached me so badly and I felt so fatigued and feverish that I couldn't resist the temptation. I have been at this desk three hours working like a slave—all school work.

I did not go uptown this afternoon as I had too much to do. Outside a driving rain has been falling for over thirty-six hours without so much as a suspicion of stopping. How I have longed for you! Last night it amounted to a positive ache. You have played me an unfair trick heart of mine; you have so completely woven yourself into the thread of my life until I cannot imagine an existence apart from you.

Paul, my dearest—honestly, it would break my heart were anything to occur to put us apart. Sometimes I catch my breath in a horrible, nameless fear, lest we should be separated.—Your loving wife.

Like the proverbs that are ingrained in the culture and mores of African societies, African poems are similarly passed from one generation to the next. This selection speaks to the joy of love and the strength of tradition.*

---

*From *African Poems and Love Songs* by Charlotte and Wolf Leslau (Mount Vernon, N.Y.: Peter Pauper Press, 1970).

Poems of Love

O how big is my beloved,
More than all the ones I know.
O how lively does my heart beat
When I only see him glow.
Love can never be forced;
Treat it fondly, it will grow.

Zanzibar

I have no hat on my head,
I have no shoes on my feet.
In what hurry I am
When I come to thee!

Ethiopia

Wedding Song

O bridegroom, rejoice!
Your bride is charming!
Your bride is a carafe,
Take care not to break her.
Lala shebo,
Lala shebo!

O listen, bride, listen:
If they ask you, you say
That you are of a good clan,
Both father and mother.
Lala shebo,
Lala shebo!

If they ask what you drink,
Tell them fresh milk and honey.
If they ask what you eat,
Tell them hump of bull.
Lala shebo,
Lala shebo!

A fast mule to ride,
A fine toga to wear.
If they can't afford these,
Kick their shins and come home.
Lala shebo,
Lala shebo!

Ethiopia

CEREMONIAL NOTES

I have spread no
snares today;
I am caught in my
love of you.

—*Egypt*

▲

Love is like a baby;
it needs to be
treated gently.

—*Congo*

This essay by educator and writer W.E.B. Du Bois is a portrait of a father's emotional upheaval as he plans his daughter Yolande's grand wedding. It first appeared in *Crisis* magazine, June 1928.

So the Girl Marries

—by W.E.B. Du Bois

FOR THE WEDDING OF
YOLANDE DU BOIS AND COUNTEE CULLEN

I remember the Boy came to me somewhat breathlessly on Christmas eve with a ring in his pocket. I told him as I had told others. "Ask her—she'll settle the matter; not I." But he was a nice boy. A rather unusual boy with the promise of fine manhood. I wished him luck. But I did not dare plead his cause. I had learned—well, I had learned.

Thus the world grew and blossomed and changed and so the Girl married. It is the end of an era—a sudden break and beginning. I rub my eyes and readjust my soul. I plan frantically. It will be a simple, quiet ceremony—

"In a church, father!"

"Oh! in a church? Of course, in a church. Well, a church wedding would be a little larger, but—"

"With Countee's father and the Reverend Frazier Miller assisting."

"To be sure—well, that is possible and, indeed, probable."

"And there will be sixteen bridesmaids."

One has to be firm somewhere—

"But, my dear! who ever heard of sixteen bridesmaids?"

"But Papa, there are eleven Moles and five indispensables and Margaret—"

Why argue? What has to be, must be; and this evidently had to be. I struggled faintly but succumbed. Now with sixteen bridesmaids and ten ushers must go at least as many invited guests.

You who in travail of soul have struggled with the devastating puzzle of selecting a small bridge party out of your total of twenty-five intimate friends, lend me your sympathy! For we faced the world-shattering problem of selecting for only two children, the friends of a pastor with twenty-five years of service in one church; and the friends of a man who knows good people in forty-five states and three continents. I may recover from it but I shall never look quite the same. I shall always have a furtive feeling in my soul. I know that at the next corner I shall meet my Best Friend and remember that I forgot to invite him. Never in all of eternity can I explain. How can I say: "Bill, I just forgot you!" Or, "My dear Mrs. Blubenski, I didn't remember where on earth you were at all or ever!" No, one can't say such things. I shall only start at them pleadingly, in doubt and pain, and slink wordlessly away.

Thirteen hundred were bidden to the marriage and no human being has one thousand three hundred friends! Five hundred came down to greet the bride at a jolly reception which I had originally planned for twenty-five. Of course, I was glad they were there. I expanded and wished for a thousand. Three thousand saw the marriage and a thousand waited on the streets. It was a great pageant; a heart-swelling throng; birds sang and Melville Charlton let the organ roll and swell beneath his quivering hands. A sweet young voice sang of Love; then came the holy:

"Freudig gefert, Ziehet dahin!"

The symbolism of that procession was tremendous. It was not the mere marriage of a maiden. It was not simply the wedding of a fine young poet. It was the symbolic march of young and black America. America, because there was Harvard, Columbia, Smith, Brown, Howard, Chicago, Syracuse, Penn and Cornell. There were three Masters of Arts and fourteen Bachelors. There were poets and teachers, actors, artists and students. But it was not simply conventional America—it had a dark and shimmering beauty all its own; a calm and high restraint and sense of new power, it was a new race; a new thought; a new thing rejoicing in a ceremony as old as the world. (And after it all and before it, such a jolly, happy crowd; some of the girls even smoked cigarettes!)

Why should there have been so much of pomp and ceremony—flowers and carriages and silk hats; wedding cake and wedding music? After all marriage in its essence is and should be very simple: a clasp of a friendly hand; a walking away together of Two who say: "Let us try to be One and face and fight a lonely world together!" What more? Is that not enough? Quite; and were I merely white I should have sought to make it end with this.

But it seems to me that I owe something extra to an Idea, a Tradition. We who are black and panting up hurried hills of hate and hindrance—we have got to establish new footholds on the slipping by-paths through which we come. They must at once be footholds of the free and the eternal, the new and the enthralled. With all of our just flouting of white convention and black religion, some things remain eternally so—Birth, Death, Pain, Mating, Children, Age. Ever and anon we must point to these truths and if the pointing be beautiful with music and ceremony or bare with silence and darkness—what matter? The width or narrowness of the gesture is a matter of choice. That one will have stripped it to the essence. It is still good and true. This soul wants color with bursting chords and scores of smiling eyes in happy raiment. It must be as this soul wills. The Girl wills this. So the Girl marries.

Part 2

To Be Wed

Marriage is an art.

HAKI MADHUBUTI

Showers and Parties

▼▼▼▼▼▼▼▼▼▼▼▼▼▼▼▼▼▼▼▼▼▼▼

Once the engagement is set, life becomes a round of celebrations and parties, lasting until the wedding. The affairs may be given by friends, siblings, coworkers, or members of the bridal party. Although the shower was once an intimate single-sex affair given by friends and family of the bride, it has become more and more a joint affair that includes men as well as women.   Nowadays, many showers are arranged around a theme. Some are lingerie parties, others are pegged to a time of day or a section of the home. But some brides are choosing celebrations that come from their cultural and ethnic heritage.   One party that has been gaining a following is the *queh-queh,* a Guyanese custom that has its origins in African tradition. Guyanese say you don't have to be invited to the wedding to come to the queh-queh. Indeed, whole villages would turn out for the often bawdy affairs filled with music, drums,

THESE HARLEM
HOOFERS INVITED
THE CHORUS TO BE
ATTENDANTS AT
THEIR WEDDING.

sensual dancing, and songs with sexual connotations. Customarily performed a week or two before a wedding, the queh-queh is closely akin to a shower given for the bride and groom, without the gifts.

In small Guyana towns of days gone by, troupes of singers, drummers, and dancers would travel from village to village to perform wherever a wedding was being planned.

The festivity is held mainly by families in the countryside of the South American country. Some affairs are held jointly for the bride and groom. But if the couple live far apart from each other, there will be separate events. In some families, it is customary for women to have a queh-queh and not men; in others, both participate.

Rejoicing and celebrating by night and resting during the day, dancers and singers would perform and the affair would continue for days, until the eve of the wedding. Invited by the family of the bride or groom, the performers would be provided room and board and paid a small price to cover their traveling expenses. If the bride's and groom's families invited different troupes, the celebration became more competitive and attendees would banter about how one group outdid the other.

Transported to the United States, queh-queh has been adapted to suit a more American time frame. The dancers may perform only two or three days before the wedding, with the biggest bash the night before. Family elders or kinsmen who hold the knowledge of the celebration are invited to bring the songs they remember and lead the crowd in singing them to the bride and groom.

Suzanne Matthews of Fort Washington, Maryland, looked forward to the pageantry of queh-queh when she married Wilfred Williams five years ago. Her family was originally from Maiconey, Guyana, and Suzanne had been living in the United States for thirteen years. "I wanted it. This was a special way for me to incorporate some of my heritage into my ceremony. I think it's important to keep up our traditional African, southern, African-American heritage. We get caught up in a superficial world. If I had done it two years after I had come, it wouldn't have been important. If I had

"A Good Night Eh" is a song that introduces the participants, dancers, and guests.

A GOOD NIGHT EH

Good night eh, good night oh,

We come for to tell you good night

Good night eh, good night oh

Good night eh, good night oh

Good night auntie, good night baby,

We come for to tell you good night.

Woman lay down and the man can't function.

CHORUS: *What kind of man is that, is that.*

Woman lay down and the man can't function.

CHORUS: *What kind of man is that, is that.*

▲

Any way Wilfred wants it, any way any way.

In the shop bridge self, any way, any way.

In the kitchen self, any way, any way.

recently come and been awed by what America had to offer, I would have thought queh-queh was backward.

"The whole way of wedding is different in Guyana," Suzanne says. Queh-queh is mostly planned by older people. In every village, there was a known person who arranged it. For example, there was Auntie Mime in the village of Maiconey. "There is the core group of people who would have people go to every queh-queh. Not everybody knows how to dance to the queh-queh. When they hear there's a queh-queh, the whole family is happy to come. It's a traditional thing they want to have done."

Suzanne's mother, Cordy E. Matthews, has been attending queh-queh since she was a child. She finds the old songs become updated with new lyrics and people add in other things. "It came from the African. It's an African dance. It's a celebration telling bride and groom what to expect when they get married and to give them a little instruction. People never spoke to children about sex. But they would tell them in song."

Suzanne agrees. "The sexual part of it is kind of instructional. Young men are not supposed to be there. It's mostly about the bride. Telling her what to expect from her husband."

Queh-queh begins with a song introducing all of the relatives or guests by calling their names in a song. The guests make a circle around the bride and groom and sing songs and circle the couple in dances. The songs, sung with exuberance, have sexual and sensual overtones. They highlight male sexual prowess and masculinity as well as feminine attributes and sexual attraction.

In some villages in Guyana, it would last three nights. The first two nights consisted of dancing and music. On the night before the wedding, the man was usually put on a chair, lifted up, and taken from his house to his fiancée's house. The dancers would follow, chanting and singing. There was special music about marriage and sex. The affair could offer some embarrassing moments as the older men offered instruction through their suggestive dances.

In some affairs, the guests lift up the bride and groom and dance around them to show how happy they are that the two families came together. In a ritual called "buying the bride," the groom searches the crowd for his fiancée. When he finds her, he calls everyone to have a look. Then the crowd lifts the bride up and sings a song asking the groom what he has come for. In other families, "buying the bride" requires her to wear a blindfold and to try to describe the actions of the crowd, who are making suggestive gestures. When she is successful, she is rewarded with money.

Loading the Bride

Like the queh-queh, a similar rite of passage is practiced in many African countries. In each village, women elders gather in a ritual called "loading the bride" to offer the woman advice and gifts to prepare her for matrimony. The celebrations, in essence, shower the bride with the supplies needed to set up a household.

Toni Comer in Columbus, Georgia, underwent the Americanized equivalent at a shower given for her by the women in her church. She sat in the middle as each woman around the room offered her a word or two of advice and encouragement about sharing finances, relationships, and love.

Many showers are arranged around a practical theme. For example, guests to a kitchen shower will bring kitchen supplies for the bride. At a "24-7" shower, each guest brings a gift that's suitable for different times of the day. Likewise a honeymoon shower would have gifts that the bride can use on her honeymoon. Coed showers that include men and women might offer gifts that the couple can share; an international shower might include gifts with a global flavor.

Shower ideas are limitless. Try an afrocentric-themed party with a jumping-the-broom luncheon. Guests should bring home-related gifts and ribbons inscribed with advice, observations, old wives' tales, or other words of wisdom and place them in a basket. The bride then draws out each ribbon and reads it to the guests, after which the ribbons are tied to a decorative broom. There will be tiny souvenir gifts for the guests, and the bride can use the broom at her wedding if she has planned to do so.

Or have a queh-queh shower. Learn some of the traditional queh-queh songs and sing them to the bride. Have each guest come up with a tip on how to make a husband happy. Serve Caribbean dishes such as cookup rice or miniature beef patties (see Selected Recipes, page 58).

Have a Kwanzaa shower. The guests could bring gifts related to the seven principles of Kwanzaa: *umoja*—unity, *kujichagulia*—self-determination, *ujima*—collective responsibility, *ujamaa*—cooperative economics, *nia*—purpose, *kuumba*—creativity, and *imani*—faith. The gifts could be goods and services made by African Americans, such as books written by or about black people, subscriptions to black magazines, or memberships at black cultural institutions. Or instead of just gifts, the guests could make promises of community-minded services such as baby-sitting for the couple or volunteering at schools, nursing homes, hospitals, or homeless shelters.

Breaking the Ice

Showers would not be complete without games that help break the ice for guests and add festivity to the gathering.

The toilet paper game is a good icebreaker: You ask people to think of their short trips to the bathrooms and the long ones, and tear off the average. You don't tell them why. When it's their turn, they tear off the first square and say their name. Then they add some detail about themselves as they tear off each square. The last one must be a wish for the new bride.

Another icebreaker is the name game. Each person says her name and the name of something she likes that begins with the first letter of her name. The next person must do the same and repeat what the previous person said. The introduction goes around the room with

the last person repeating what everyone else has said. Everyone is allowed to help with hints, especially if the crowd is a large one.

OTHER SHOWER GAMES

Mama said: Each person must dig into her purse and pull out an item to describe how to make a good marriage, without using the word marriage.

He said she said: A good game for a coed affair. The

hostess calls in advance to find out information about the couple, their relationship, likes and dislikes, habits, how and where they met, how long they have been dating, what they like to eat, what their hobbies are, and so on. The men compete against the women. The men answer trivia questions about the bride and the women answer questions about the groom. The side with the most points wins the game.

Black trivia game: This game can be very involved, but once you have compiled all the information, it may be used again at other parties. Using fan magazines, newspaper articles, gossip, television shows, and other sources, compile a list of facts and curious details about popular black figures, celebrities, or sports stars. For example, Michael Jordan plays for what team? Divide the group into teams, depending on how many guests there are. Each person gets points for correct answers. The person with the most points wins.

Purse scavenger hunt: The guests are provided a list of items that they must find, but only in their purse. Each item receives a certain number of points. For example, a hairpin would get 5 points, a comb might get 5, an afro pick might get 20 points, or a condom would get 100 points. The person with the most points wins.

Finding the Words

Invitations

In many Caribbean and African countries, invitations to a wedding were often oral. In some African societies, a family elder was appointed to oversee the inviting of guests and the preparations to receive the wedding guests. The announcement was passed from family member to family member by word of mouth. However, some people who were not part of the extended family and friends would receive formal handwritten invitations. In small villages, it was easy to let the next-door neighbor know about the upcoming festivities. Words would pass from one villager to the next, and they would then join in the preparations for the wedding. In today's society, with families and friends more scattered and considerations of time more pressing, the written invitation is generally a more efficient way of spreading the word. And while it is always an option to rely on established wording in invitations, many couples now want to plumb cultural depths to find words that are more meaningful and culturally appropriate for the community invited to the affair they are creating.

In selecting the wording for your invitations, thank-you cards, or wedding programs, you will notice that European tradition invites the guests to witness the wedding ceremony. But an afrocentric affair will expect more from its wedding community. Those who attend weddings with an African sensibility are asked to be more involved in the affair. The wedding is considered the sacred space that joins families and helps to strengthen them. Guests are not to be simply passive witnesses; as part of the couple's extended family, they are charged to actively support and sanction the couple's undertaking, according to Evanston, Illinois, wedding planner Deborah Lewis-Kearns, who has written vows and invitation wording for many affairs that she has helped plan. The wedding ceremony is considered a transforming ritual that completes the circle of life, one that brings families, ancestors, and progeny together for a celebration.

In the past, the wedding invitation followed European formality and rules of etiquette. Today, those formalities are more relaxed so couples may find a balance between their desire for convention and personal expression. Not only is an invitation a way to provide information about the nuptials, it can also be a way to saturate the affair with a particular ambience. The invitations can help prepare the guests for what may be for many their first cultural wedding experience. They will include envelopes, invitations, reception cards, and response-card envelopes as well as small maps for out-of-town guests and other instructions and announcements.

In addition to basic information—date and time of the affair, names of those hosting the wedding, full names of the bride and groom, location of the ceremony and reception, phone numbers, response card—the invitation can offer a more personal and individual forum for expression. The following are examples of wording that can be used for wedding invitations.

ISSUED BY BOTH FAMILIES

Two hearts merging
to expand the circle of our family
Mr. and Mrs. James
and Mr. and Mrs. Jones
ask that you share their joy
in an African cultural wedding ceremony
as we join our families
in the marriage of Imani James and Gyasi Jones
on Saturday, the 11th of September
One thousand nine hundred and ninety-six
at 2 o'clock
First Baptist Church
201 W. Main St.
Atlanta, Ga.
Please respond by September 1st

ISSUED BY BOTH FAMILIES

In the spirit of our African-American heritage,
we join hands with past, present, and future
Mr. and Mrs. James
and Mr. and Mrs. Jones
ask you to share with us as we witness
the vows of marriage between
Imani James and Gyasi Jones

ISSUED BY THE BRIDE'S PARENTS

Mr. and Mrs. Robert Jones
request the honor of your presence
at the African-inspired ceremony
joining our daughter Imani James
in matrimony with Gyasi Jones
Please join us to share this sacred moment
broadening our circle of family and friends

ISSUED BY THE COUPLE

Through others we are somebody
Imani James and Gyasi Jones
invite you to join our family circle
as we celebrate the uniting
of our families in marriage
Our ceremony will joyfully honor our heritage
in a cultural rite that combines our African and
American traditions

FROM THE COUPLE

We rejoice in the celebration
uniting our families
at the marriage of
Imani James
and Gyasi Jones
Your presence is requested
and your support will enrich us
throughout our marital journey

FROM THE COUPLE

Imani James
and Gyasi Jones
invite you to join us to witness our commitment
to each other as we jump the broom
into the land of holy matrimony
on Saturday, the 11th of September
One thousand nine hundred and ninety-six
at 2 o'clock
Eastern Star Hall
201 W. Main St.
Atlanta, Ga.

1971–1996
Shirley and Bob Smith
Come share with us as we celebrate
25 years of love and devotion.
We are delighted to renew our vows
in an African-inspired service

FROM ONE PARENT

With a joyful heart
Ann B. James
welcomes you to the celebration
that joins her daughter Imani James
in marriage to Gyasi Jones
As in the African tradition,
we see this sacred moment as a uniting of
families

Please respond

A wedding feast
follows the ceremony
at the Eastern Star Hall
25 W. Broad St.
Philadelphia, Pa.

Feel free to include other information in the envelope with the invitation. Include places of interest for people who are visiting for a few days and who might want something to do while they are in town. Include the names and price ranges of restaurants in the area, black sites of note, shopping suggestions, and safety tips if necessary. Also include details about your wedding ceremony if it has some special or unique feature. It will help familiarize the guests with the proceedings. Some brides start a wedding newsletter filled with details about their wedding plans, such as a prewedding barbecue for early arrivals and tips for the guests.

The Wedding Program

A wedding program will include the order of service, names of members of the wedding party, date, time, and place of the wedding, as well as other details of interest in the ceremony. Here you might want to include the appropriate responses for parts of your ceremony. Here are a few ideas:

> We are proud to announce that our ceremony is inspired by the traditional Yoruba ceremony of Nigeria, which offers the tasting of several spices, including kola nut, sugar, salt, and honey. As in the Yoruba tradition, this ritual is shared with family and friends of the village. Feel free to have a taste as a symbol of your support for Gyasi and Imani. There will be singers, dancers, and drummers. In an African ceremony, rejoicing is spontaneous, so feel free to move with the spirit by clapping your hands.

> As in African-American ceremonies, call and response is an integral part of the celebration. Feel to respond "ashe" (ah-shay) where you might say amen.

> Immediately following the ceremony, please stand at your seats as we will have an old-fashioned broom jumping. The ritual, handed down from generation to generation, reminds us that when our vows were not legally sanctioned during slavery, we sought the legitimacy of matrimony by jumping the broom. For our ancestors, this small

ritual was a legal and binding act that, in their eyes, helped to hold families together and allowed them to create a moment of dignity and strength.

Saying Thanks

After all the showers and wedding gifts and other acts of kindness during your wedding, you, of course, want to thank the people who thought of you. Here are some ways:

Our ceremony blends aspects of our culture and our heritage—the Caribbean-American and African. Thank you for joining our village of family, extended family, and friends. We are grateful for your love, guidance, and support and appreciate your generous gift.

We pay homage to our ancestors, whose shoulders we stand on and whose wisdom helps shine a guiding light on our past, present, and future. Our celebration was enriched by your presence. We thank you for your generosity.

The Ceremony

Hiring a Wedding Coordinator

In many African societies, the role of wedding coordinator was performed by elder women who were close and trusted relatives of the bride. This person would instruct the bride as to the customs and traditions and offer sexual instruction, as well as oversee invitations, plans for the feast, and the trousseau. On our shores, similarly, the coordinator was an aunt, older sister, or grandmother who had a flair for detail as well as a drill sergeant's control. But with more women busier than ever, a professional might be the necessary choice. A wedding coordinator might manage all the details of your wedding from start to finish or just coordinate on your wedding day. She will help you select your dress, address cards and invitations, prepare a menu, or simply hold your hand on the big day. Have a contract that outlines exactly what you expect from the consultant and exactly what areas are covered by her fees. This person can charge by the hour, fix a rate based on the cost of your wedding, or charge a flat rate.

Some churches have a person assigned to help brides with their wedding plans. Some bridal shop owners double as wedding planners. Some wedding planners are also event planners. Choose a planner who has had several years of experience in weddings. She should be familiar with all the possible catastrophes—large and small—that can happen during a wedding.

Have an idea about how you would like your wedding structured. Do you want the standard affair—bride escorted by father, given to the groom—or something less conventional? If you want a more afrocentric wedding, choose someone who has experience in African traditions. A consultant should be comfortable handling a variety of weddings.

A bridal consultant may speak with the minister about the church's rules. She is a good source of information on caterers, limousine services, dressmakers, and tuxedo rentals. And it is helpful to have an experienced neutral participant during a wedding, particularly when emotions overtake reason during the planning stage.

Select a planner who can be flexible and not impose her point of view on your affair. A wedding planner should offer suggestions based on what you want and need. Be sure to ask for references from at least three brides who have used the consultant's services.

Selecting an Officiant

Most brides will choose their own pastor to perform their wedding ceremony. But those who want a more afrocentric ceremony might look elsewhere for clergy or a spiritual leader who has experience conducting a ceremony with the ambience of African tradition. In addition, this person should be licensed in your state to perform a wedding ceremony. If not, your wedding will require someone who can legally pronounce you husband and wife.

Be prepared to explain to your minister about the aspects of an afrocentric ceremony. Do a little research. Be specific about the rit-

1 Year in Advance

Begin saving.

Consult a wedding planner, if necessary.

6–12 Months in Advance

Begin premarital counseling.

Meet with clergy.

Discuss wedding plans with parents.

Reserve wedding, reception, and honeymoon sites.

Plan general details.

Select a florist.

Choose attendants.

Shop for dress, accessories, suit.

Set up bridal registry at stores.

3 Months in Advance

Order passports.

Order invitations, announcements.

Choose transportation for the wedding party.

Order dresses; have alterations done.

Choose photographer and videographer.

Have medical exams done.

Choose a band or disc jockey.

Plan ceremony and reception.

Meet with caterer, musician.

6–8 Weeks
in Advance

Mail invitations.

Plan lodging for
guests.

Have portraits taken.

Choose gifts for
attendants.

Submit list to
photographer.

Submit requests to
musicians.

Have final dress
fittings.

Plan rehearsal
dinner.

Obtain wedding
rings.

2 Weeks
in Advance

Get marriage license.

Make beauty
appointment.

Check honeymoon
reservations.

Purchase traveler's
checks (if using).

1 Week in Advance

Pack for
honeymoon.

Address
announcements.

Check final details.

Have rehearsal
dinner.

Get hair done.

uals you want to include—libation, naming ceremony, tasting of spices. Be prepared to explain the cultural genesis of these rituals. Although more and more ministers and spiritual advisers are increasingly open about African rituals, some might decline to participate in a ceremony that they are unfamiliar with.

It might require more research to find someone to officiate in an afrocentric ceremony. If you don't know anyone with experience in African-influenced weddings, get referrals from friends and acquaintances who have had such weddings. Ask organizers of cultural events or members of black cultural centers for referrals to folks who have had this experience. Ask black bridal consultants for referrals. Black studies departments of colleges in your area might be another good source for an officiant. Be prepared to pay a fee.

Creating a Sacred Space

If you decide to hold your wedding outside a church, you might want to find a place that creates a sacred space. In African tradition, groves, forests, waterfalls, lakes, rivers, mountains, and other places where heaven meets earth were regarded as a place where God dwells. You might want to have a ceremony like that of Ann and Chester Grundy, who married in a park in Birmingham, Alabama. Or like that of Shirley Williams Kirksey and Gary Kirksey, whose West Virginia wedding included taking their guests by boat to Blennerhassett Island for an outdoor affair. The reception took place aboard the river craft.

Although rain at a wedding is considered a blessing, you will need to make backup plans if you choose nature as a backdrop!

Selected Recipes

Cookup Rice

1½ cups dried black-eyed peas, presoaked

2 garlic cloves, chopped

4 cups water

1 medium onion, chopped

2 cups unsweetened coconut milk

2 scallions, chopped

1 celery rib, chopped

1 teaspoon dried thyme

Salt and ground black pepper to taste

2 cups uncooked rice

Combine the peas, garlic, water, and onion. Cook until almost tender. Add the coconut milk, scallions, celery, thyme, salt, and pepper. Cover and bring to a boil. Add the rice and stir. Cook over low heat until the liquid is absorbed and the rice is tender.

Conch Fritters

1 pound conch (2 or 3 of the shellfish), ground

4 ounces chopped onion

3 ounces chopped celery

3 ounces chopped sweet pepper

⅛ teaspoon hot pepper (optional)

1 teaspoon thyme

6 ounces chopped ripe tomato or 1 ounce tomato paste

1 cup water

2½ pounds flour

4 teaspoons baking powder

½ teaspoon salt

1 quart cooking oil

Grind the first 7 ingredients together and place in a large mixing bowl. Stir in the water, then add the flour, baking powder, and salt. Mix until the batter is slightly stiff.

Add the oil to a 2-quart pot. Bring to a sizzle. Test the heat with small portion of batter.

Turn the heat to medium. Use a tablespoon to measure portions
of fritter. Drop in oil and cook until medium brown. Remove
with a strainer. Drain on paper towels. Serve hot.

LOBSTER SALAD

*3 cups cooked, chopped lobster
    meat*

1 cup cooked baby shrimp

*2 tablespoons finely chopped
    shallots*

1 cup chopped celery

½ cup chopped sweet red peppers

*2 hard-boiled eggs, 1 chopped,
    1 sliced*

*½ cup mayonnaise, or more as
    needed*

¼ teaspoon paprika

Salt and black pepper to taste

Lettuce, for garnish

Lobster claws, for garnish

Olives, for garnish

Put lobster, shrimp, shallots, celery, sweet peppers, chopped egg,
mayonnaise, and seasonings into a bowl and mix until well
blended. Arrange lettuce in a serving bowl, spoon salad onto
lettuce, and garnish with lobster claws, egg slices, and olives.
Serves six.

FRIED PLANTAINS

1 cup olive oil

3 black ripe plantains

Heat oil in heavy frying pan. Slice plantains diagonally. Cook them
in oil until they are crisp and brown. Drain on paper towels.
Serve in a bowl on a bed of lettuce.

Plantains may also be baked in the oven. Heat the oven to 350° F.
Spray cooking oil on a cookie sheet. Arrange plantains on
cookie sheet. Cook until golden brown and crisp.

GROUPER FINGERS

1 cup cooking oil
½ cup cornmeal
¼ cup flour
1 teaspoon oregano

½ teaspoon cayenne pepper
Salt and black pepper to taste
Grouper fillets, cut into strips

Heat oil in a heavy frying pan.
In plastic bag, shake cornmeal and flour and seasonings until well
mixed. Add 2 or 3 grouper strips and shake until well coated.
Cook grouper until golden brown on both sides.
Drain on paper towels and serve hot.

MINIATURE BEEF PATTIES

Miniature spiced beef patties can be purchased in the frozen-foods
section of most grocery stores or in Caribbean specialty stores.

LOW COUNTRY CRAB BOIL

2 pounds smoked sausage or
kielbasa, cut into bite-sized
pieces
2 pounds baby red potatoes in
skin
6 ears of corn, cut in half
2 large onions, cut in chunks

2 stalks celery, coarsely chopped
Old Bay Seasoning
4 garlic cloves
2 pounds of shrimp
6 crab, cooked and cut in half

In a large pot of water, boil sausage until done. Add vegetables,
seasoning, and garlic cloves and cook until potatoes are nearly
done. Add shrimp and crab and cook until shrimp turn pink.
Serve in bowls with crusty bread.

COLESLAW

3 cups shredded cabbage

1 cup shredded carrot

1 cup chopped red onion

1/3 cup sugar

1 cup mayonnaise

4 tablespoons lemon juice

1 teaspoon celery seed

Salt and black pepper to taste

In a bowl, mix ingredients together thoroughly. Chill for one hour before serving. Serves six.

RED RICE

4 slices bacon

1 cup chopped onion

1 cup chopped bell pepper

2 cloves chopped garlic

2 bay leaves

1½ cups rice

1½ cups crushed tomatoes

Salt and pepper to taste

Cook bacon in large pan until crisp and remove. Pour off half the fat. In remaining fat, cook onion, pepper, and garlic until tender. Add remaining ingredients. Stir. Bring to a boil. Turn down heat and simmer until rice is tender.

COLLARD GREEN QUICHE

3 large eggs

1 cup milk

1 small onion, chopped

2 tablespoons butter

10 ounces (bunch or package) fresh collard greens, washed, chopped, blanched, and steamed

Salt, nutmeg, and ground pepper to taste

2–3 strips cooked bacon or turkey bacon, crumbled

¼ cup grated sharp Cheddar cheese

¼ cup grated mozzarella cheese

1 deep-dish pie shell

Using the eggs and milk, make a custard. Set aside.

Preheat the oven to 375° F.

Sauté the onion in the butter. Add the greens and stir until tender. Add seasonings and blend into the custard. Add most of the bacon. Layer the cheeses in the pie shell, reserving some for the top. Pour the custard mixture into the shell. Top with the remaining grated cheese and crumbled bacon. Bake about 35 to 40 minutes, until puffed and brown.

Frozen collards can be used, but heat and drain well before preparations.

Bahamian Fruit Punch

4 cups pineapple juice

1 cup crushed pineapple

2 cups mango juice

1 cup lemon juice

1 bottle club soda

1 cup sugar

Lemon slices

Mix ingredients in punch bowl. Chill until ready to serve. Makes about 4 quarts.

Strawberry Iced Tea Punch

Fresh strawberries, sliced

Sugar to taste

4 cups brewed strawberry tea

3 cups apple juice

2 cups sweetened lemonade

Lemon slices

Mix fresh strawberries with sugar and freeze in small cups. Combine remaining ingredients and refrigerate until chilled. Add punch to frozen strawberries in punch bowl.

CEREMONIAL NOTES

Before the wedding ceremony in Nigeria, an Ibo woman would visit her husband's family and sweep out their home.

▲

In Senegal, the bride wears white and gold—white to symbolize her purity and gold to symbolize her value.

▲

On leaving her house, a South African bride will pass under an arch of branches while a libation is poured.

▲

If a man does not find his bride a virgin, it's a big deal in Haiti. The day after the wedding night he opens all the doors and windows in the house. And he would then buy a square loaf of bread and remove the inside.

Ambrosia

2 cups pineapple, cut into chunks

10 seedless oranges, peeled and sliced with membranes removed

2 sliced bananas

3 cups shredded coconut

1/2 cup sugar

In a large bowl, gently combine ingredients, reserving some orange slices and coconut for garnish. Sprinkle the top with the remaining coconut flakes and orange slices. Refrigerate until ready to serve.

BLACK WEDDING CAKE

In yesteryear, Olwen Gillman's mother used to grind all the ingredients for the black cake—raisins, nuts, currants, candied fruits, and citron. She'd set them in a crock filled with port wine or rum and let it ferment. Then she'd put the mixture into a container with port wine for *months* before using. It took six months to set. She burned sugar to make it black and prepared the batter, pouring it into baking pans lined with brown paper bags cut to fit the pans. Lard was used to grease the pans before baking. After the cake was baked, a small portion of liquor would be drizzled over it each week to maintain softness and moisture.

Olwen's mother made the cake—in a triangle shape—for her wedding to Edwin. His mother helped to ice it—and that alone took a week.

For a black cake, cooks use the richest ingredients, butter, and sugar to symbolize the rich investment that is a marriage, says M. A. Mathias, an anthropologist and expert on Caribbean wedding traditions. They use fruit that is hard to get to symbolize the precious relationship between bride and groom as well as a wish for prosperity and fruitfulness. Letting the liquor set for months symbolizes the longevity of marriage.

BLACK WEDDING CAKE

½ pound seeded raisins, halved
  (optional)

1 pound sultana raisins

¼ pound currants

½ cup rum, brandy, or sherry

½ pound pitted dates

⅛ pound candied lemon peel

⅛ pound candied orange peel

⅓ pound candied pineapple

½ pound candied cherries,
  halved

¼ pound candied citron

¼ pound chopped walnuts

2 cups sifted flour

½ teaspoon each cinnamon,
  cloves, mace

½ teaspoon baking powder

1 cup white sugar

1 cup brown sugar

¼ pound butter, creamed

5 eggs

1 tablespoon orange juice

1 teaspoon almond extract

1 tablespoon rose water
  (optional)

Soak the raisins and currants in the liquor for 1 hour.

Cut the dates, peels, pineapple, cherries, and citron into paper-thin strips. Combine with the nuts, sprinkle with 1 cup of the flour, and mix well.

To the remaining flour add the spices and baking powder. Sift together. In a large mixing bowl, gradually add the sugars to the butter. Cream well, then beat in the eggs, one at a time.

Combine the juice, extract, and rose water, if using. Add to the bowl alternately with the sifted dry ingredients and soaked raisins and currants. Blend in the fruit strips and nuts.

Heavily grease pans with a mixture of two parts shortening and one part flour. Pour the batter into the pans two-thirds full. Bake in a very slow oven until a cake tester in the center comes out clean. Cool and wrap. Let the cake cool in the pan before removing.

There are many variations in preparing the black cake. The fruit may be soaked for a longer time, up to one month. Combine the butter and sugar from the beginning of making the batter.

In Petit Martinique on the island of Grenada, a feast was first given by the bridegroom, then a week later one was given by the bride. After the church ceremony, the couple would walk to the reception through the crowd. The guests would then go on to receptions in both homes. Everyone would have to visit the home of the groom and have cake and wine, then the home of the bride for a feast. As the couple walked, there would be string music and people would come and kiss them on the way and give them a silver coin, a shilling. By the time they got to where they were going, they would have collected many coins.

Beat all five eggs and set aside until needed with the extracts that are used. Buy the candied fruits already diced. You can use cake flour that is already sifted. If cake flour is used, there is no need for baking powder.

A BLACK CAKE

Knocking, Asking, Taking

The ties established between two families by a happy marriage are stronger than those of wealth.

AFRICAN PROVERB

Customs from Around the World

▼ ▼

Reflections on Marriage

Despite our modern attitudes, the reasons for entering the state of matrimony have remained unchanged. Marriage confirms our family traditions. It is a spiritual rite of passage that links us to our ancestors and joins us with our descendants. It doesn't happen in a vacuum. It is not a solitary event. It is a celebration that intensifies our desire to unite with someone else. Marriage cements families, builds nations, and strengthens the community. It preserves and upholds cultural beliefs, social institutions, and value systems.   Marriage is a source of strength and continuity, says Morris Jeff, a social worker and spiritual adviser in New Orleans, who has widely studied African rituals and traditions. "It is unifying the connection between the generations of the race. The act of marriage is an act of remembrance. The original call is for us to be in unity with ourselves. You don't *start* a family when you get married, you *join* a family. In its relationships, you are broadening the base of the extended family, bringing a oneness to everything and everyone that lived before us —now one full family together. The act of marriage is a rejoining, a remembering, a recalling of the unity."

The rituals applied in a wedding ceremony are a culmination of ancient customs used through the generations. They may often seem quaint, and to some even archaic, but they have endured nearly intact, with only a few modern touches. The rituals in this chapter are intended to help rediscover that familial link—with the Africans, the middle-passage voyagers, the slaves and freedmen whose love for one another and strength have brought us this far so that the cycle may be repeated.

Marriage is a rite of passage; according to an African proverb, "It is the well from which we all drink." Marriage is an essential ritual; it indicates that you are looking out not just for yourself, but for your family. The merging of two families helps to give children stability and parameters, says the Rev. Emmanuel F. Y. Grantson of Christ Ascension Lutheran Church in Philadelphia.

Getting married is a journey rather than a destination. The beginning is the maze that the ceremonies and rituals help to map. Well-known and time-tested rites serve as an emotional anchor during the upheavals that accompany each of life's milestones. Engagements are vulnerable periods on the threshold of married status. Deciding to take a mate results in a shift of family and community relationships. The certainties in life seem to ebb and flow with the adrenaline of passions during this courtship period. The words spoken during ancient rituals serve as incantations to help ward off evil and unhappiness and to conjure up tranquility, health, and truth. Marriage rituals help to transform single and independent people into a single dependent unit. They offer a smooth path to a new station in life. The wedding ceremony confirms the couple's new position and their ties to the community.

Building on Tradition

When Ann and Chester Grundy got married in Birmingham, Alabama, in 1974, they combined the history of the civil rights movement, the birthday of black nationalist Marcus Garvey, ancient rituals of Africa, and the holiday of Kwanzaa to create their version of an African ceremony.

The couple interviewed friends from countries across the continent of Africa to learn more about marriage customs there. They were concerned because they knew nothing about the African village from which their forebears may have originated. But they were undeterred. Since their lack of knowledge opened doors to the entire continent, they decided to borrow from Africa's many traditions.

Not only did they want a ceremony steeped in tradition, they wanted one that yielded to family heritage as well. As a child of a well-known minister, Ann knew the hometown that had nurtured her would offer the perfect setting for the ceremony. Birmingham was a flash point during the civil rights era. She had grown up near the site of the 1963 bombing of the 16th Street Baptist Church. She had played in the park where Bull Connor let loose his hoses on early civil rights demonstrators. She chose the park as the site for her wedding on a culturally significant day—Garvey's birthday, August 17.

Their celebration, they decided, would reflect the African belief that a wedding is a community event. As early celebrators of Kwanzaa, they incorporated the tenets of the Nguzo Saba, the celebration's seven guiding principles based on African life and society, into the ceremony. It encompassed a family reunion that would welcome Chester's family members and reunite Ann's many brothers and sisters who had spread out across the United States.

The community enthusiastically joined in the plans. Family and friends offered their talents from preparing the food to creating the decorations. Ann's brothers and sisters made the musical arrangements. Neighbors offered to put up family and friends for the occasion. A clothing designer from California made Ann's dress from a colorful Senegalese fabric. Ann had commissioned it sight unseen, but she said it was perfect. The morning before the wedding, her brothers went out to the park with mops and buckets to clean the area. A team of homeless people pitched in to help clean and set up chairs. An artist set up a display of his work.

The weeklong celebration was an event attended by nearly eight hundred people, many dressed in African garb. For most, it was the

ANN AND CHESTER GRUNDY'S 1974 WEDDING IN BIRMINGHAM, ALABAMA, INCLUDED VOWS BASED ON KWANZAA'S SEVEN GUIDING PRINCIPLES.

first time they had experienced an afrocentric wedding. A spiritual leader offered a libation, the ceremony incorporated gongs, drummers, and dancers, and the couple passed a unity cup through the crowd.

The wedding, Ann said, took on a life of its own. "It allowed people to participate to enhance the experience. It took the attention off me and put it on the bringing together of black people. It was more than a wedding ceremony."

Today, many more African-American couples have decided they want more ethnically from their weddings. They are seeking a more meaningful way to seal their marital vows. They are aware of how fragile relationships are in these modern times, and many weigh seriously the commitment being made before family and friends. They long to make their special day reflect their ethnicity in much the same way Jewish couples will step under the huppah, or the way Chinese couples will wear traditional silk garments in red and gold, or those of Latino and Italian heritage will perform the dollar dance.

Unfortunately for many people of African descent, many of those essential family-enriching rituals have been lost during the voyage through the middle passage, slavery, and integration.

Even many blacks of Caribbean descent who once prided themselves on their family traditions have let go of practices their elders once held dear. For example, in the Virgin Islands, it was customary for the wedding announcement—banns—to be issued in church a few weeks before the nuptials. Weddings were formal affairs in which a prospective groom had to write a letter to a young woman's parents to request permission to court their daughter, says Guy Benjamin, a retired principal from the island of St. John. The parents would signal their permission, also in writing. The groom was then required to build a house for his bride before the wedding.

The young man would visit with his intended at every occasion and her family would become acquainted with him. Although formal invitations were mailed to acquaintances, all neighbors and friends were notified by word of mouth. The wedding party arrived at the ceremony by sailboat, traveling from the other islands.

Similarly in Haiti, as recently as the 1960s, the marriage proposal or "letter of application" would be made in writing to the parents of the bride. Composed in formal French, it would be printed on decorative paper, wrapped in silk, and delivered by a member of the prospective groom's family.

However, many African-American couples are now making an effort to rediscover and re-create their spiritual and ancestral past. They now acknowledge and accept the riches of their forgotten African heritage to link their future with their past, sometimes combining the African and the American parts of their heritage as a monument to the bittersweet legacy of their ancestors.

This interest in African traditions had its genesis in the 1960s, a period in which expressions of black pride and cultural consciousness exploded on the national scene. Scholars began to examine their lifestyles and take from African tradition to create daily routines that offered some a meaningful alternative to an American culture. Kwanzaa was created in 1966 by Maulana Ron Karenga as a cultural alternative to what some felt was a commercialization of Christmas. As black students and scholars began to visit Africa in significant numbers, and many Africans came to study in the United States, a cultural exchange began to evolve on college campuses and a black revolutionary spirit flourished.

By the 1970s, many African Americans began to follow the lead of couples like the Grundys, and Haki and Safisha Madhubuti, whose African wedding was covered by *Jet* magazine, and began to incorporate African traditions in education, cultural celebrations, and social interactions to create what they felt was a more honest reflection of their heritage. They became involved in developing philosophies about black families, which included and embraced marriage ceremonies—the foundation of the family and society.

The early ceremonies encompassed many elements that are retained today, including a drum call, libation, exchange of vows,

recitation of the Nguzo Saba, parental words of wisdom, singing, dancing, and feasting.

By the end of the 1970s, interest in such cultural expressions waned, only to resurface in the mid-1980s, a period when the world began to focus attention on the struggle for freedom in South Africa. Black History Week celebrations expanded to a month; a multicultural movement embraced and accepted ethnic differences. We began to call ourselves African Americans, and Kwanzaa began to be a popular celebration during the winter holiday season.

Today, we are seeing an evolutionary turn toward tradition, says Philadelphia's Rev. Emmanuel Grantson. A native of Ghana, he says it is natural that African-American couples would want to incorporate the ancient traditions of their foreparents. African Americans are experiencing a collective resurgence of the ancestral memory in which rituals are not divorced from life but are an integral part of it.

Grantson has presided over more and more afrocentric weddings in the past few years. His ceremonies, tailor-made for each couple, are based on Scripture, contextualized and spiced with homilies and ancient African proverbs, stories that provide a moral basis for marriage. According to Grantson, these rituals allow African Americans to follow in the path set by their ancestors—to move with nature. They provide guidance and structure to everyday life. Each ritual, large and small, offers instruction in the natural flow of life. His ceremonies encourage exuberant participation by the guests, who are considered an integral part of the wedding. The minister will say "Agoo"—give me your attention, and the congregation responds "Ameh"—you have our attention. The ceremonies include dancers, drummers, and singers, sacred rites and public exhortation.

The Rev. Reuben S. Conner of the Urban Evangelical Mission in Texas says he has seen a similar renaissance among the weddings he has presided over. "More and more people are concerned about how their foreparents did it. Couples are researching church tradition and incorporating that into the wedding."

Conner, who presided over a wedding that re-created a slave broomstick-jumping ceremony, said couples are doing meticulous research. Some are getting wedding ideas and traditions from three generations back while others are putting a little from each generation into their wedding ceremony or are involving as many family members, particularly the elders, in their ceremonies as they can. "One of our traditions is to involve as many generations of parents as possible," he says. "Have them participate in a significant way. Put an emphasis on the procession before and after wedding."

Conner says many relatives and family elders participate by marching in a formal procession and being seated with the family at the front of the church. Many couples are having the elders' names printed in programs with their ages and explaining their relationship to the groom or bride.

Linda Humes of Yaffa Productions in New York City offers cultural ceremonies involving traditions from the Caribbean, Africa, and the United States. The Caribbean wedding parties that she plans may include stilt walkers, steel bands, and calypso music as well as the Yoruba tasting of spices. Although most couples don't know much about many of these cultural traditions, she says, they want to take ownership of their heritage. But she says some ministers have been reluctant to officiate at ceremonies that deviate from religious practices with the use of libations or spice tasting. She will often help explain the origins of the many rituals. "We'll talk to the minister and explain that the belief is in God."

For Carolyn White-Washington, the quest for cultural significance encouraged her to combine her Southern sensibilities and her fiancé William Washington's afrocentric attitude in a ceremony that embraced African and African-American traditions. Taking cues from African traditions, their engagement included approaching family elders to ask permission to marry. Their afrocentric-design invitations let people know that there was going to be something unique about the service. William dressed in full African attire, while Carolyn wore the traditional American white dress and veil. Their ceremony, by Rev. Willie Wilson at the African-centered Union Temple Baptist Church in Washington, D.C., opened with a drum call to signal the start of the ceremony. A libation was poured and the couple were administered the symbols of life. These were hoe, which represents self-sufficiency; pot, representing food; broom, symbolizing cleanliness; honey, symbolizing sweetness of marriage; shield, for protection of the home; spear, for defense of the home; wine, which represents ancestral spirits; wheat, a symbol of fertility; salt, an essential ingredient of life; pepper, symbolizing reconciliation; bitter herb, for the growing pains of marriage; and water, an essential force of life.* Carolyn rubbed a fertility doll to ensure that

---

*From online African Wedding Guide, http://www.melanet.com/melanet/wedding/wed.html

the couple would be blessed with children. They lit unity candles, and her grandfather said grace at the reception.

Heidi Hamilton and her fiancé, Damon D. Caldwell, decided to write their vows. They wrote words that reflected their feelings and wishes for their marriage. They included sentiments about being supportive and a willingness to exercise and lead a healthy lifestyle. They emphasized the importance of honesty in their relationship as well as talking things out. They vowed to be together "until love is no more." The ceremony was held on August 28, 1992, the anniversary of the civil rights march on Washington. It included a reading of words by the Rev. Dr. Martin Luther King Jr., as well as a poem by Maya Angelou. Both Heidi's parents escorted her down the aisle. An opening and closing libation was poured to honor their grandparents and ancestors from both families, with exhortations of "ashe" from the guests. At the reception, both fathers were given a showcase in which to speak of their feelings.

A Jewish Ceremony

LaDonna and Gerald Brown of Chicago took their July 1995 marriage back to ancient Jewish traditions. LaDonna, formerly Baptist, converted to Judaism shortly before their wedding. A week before the ceremony, the couple stood before two witnesses to sign a ketubah, a contractual agreement that has traditionally been an essential part of the Jewish wedding ritual. The document, similar to today's prenuptial agreement, outlined their specific responsibilities to each other as husband and wife. It is read by the rabbi, and explained to the bride and groom so that there will be no surprises.

In ancient times, the ketubah was a contract that protected Jewish women. It ensured that a wife would not be treated as a slave and would be protected if her husband decided to leave. It also protected a wife's assets and the worldly possessions that she brought to a marriage. It specified how the husband would provide for her, the dowry she would bring, and other gifts to be given her, as well as how the property would be dispensed in case of divorce.

At the ceremony, performed in English and Hebrew by Rabbi Capers C. Funnye Jr., the bride and groom stood under the huppah, a canopy that symbolizes the house they will build and share together. The rabbi led LaDonna around the groom seven times, as she recited *"Ahnee muchan, ahnee muchan"*—"I will obey, I will obey."

The couple shared three glasses of wine, which seal the various affirmations—the seven blessings for the marriage. The ketubah was read before the congregation. The vows were given, consummated with the giving of a ring. As Gerald placed the ring on LaDonna's finger, he vowed, "Be thou my wife in accordance with the laws of Moses and the people of Israel. I will faithfully love and cherish you." Then Gerald smashed the glass that they drank from, indicating that what they share must be held sacred.

Renewing Cultural Covenants

In Ghana and other parts of Africa, a marriage is considered an alliance between families and not a decision made by two lovers. Historically, the woman had little choice because many marriages were often arranged at childhood by the families. Wedding rituals in the motherland incorporating an elaborate courting ritual still form a common thread among many African countries. When a young man finds the woman he wants to marry, it requires a series of negotiations, often over several weeks, between his family and hers. Once the negotiations are settled, the bride recedes into seclusion, being pampered and protected until, upon the day of her wedding, she is accompanied by an entourage of female family members to the house of her fiancé's family, where the marriage is consummated.

According to African tradition, any marriage not involving the family is not recognized, and that couple is seen as living in sin. Today, many African families hold two ceremonies, a traditional one

LADONNA AND
GERALD BROWN
WERE MARRIED
IN A JEWISH
CEREMONY IN
CHICAGO.

to satisfy the family and the ancestors, and another to satisfy religious leaders. Rev. Grantson says there is no reason not to blend both traditions into one ceremony. We carry ritual in ourselves. What ritual does is transform; ceremonies merely confirm.

Like most customs and traditions around the world, the marriage ceremony in Africa varies from family to family and from country to country. But according to Pastor Grantson there are three basic components to a traditional African wedding: knocking, asking, and taking.

Because family ties and compatibility are considered more important than love, the ceremonial "knocking" includes a full confidential investigation on the part of both families. It might take three months or up to a year. The family elders want to find out whether the girl is religious. Does she know the meaning of an oath? What village is she from? They want to find out whether the boy is responsible. Does he have a job?

According to *African Marriage Customs and Church Law* by the Rev. Father Joe Chuks Atado, once an acceptable bride is found, the groom's father may request a trusted friend or a family elder to act as an emissary in the arrangements. Usually a father, grandfather, or uncle, this person must undertake a detailed investigation of the woman and her family and report back with his findings. If they are satisfactory, he will accompany the groom and his family to meet with the woman's family for the betrothal. The emissary is charged with delivering the matrimonial gifts—often liquor and money— and he guides the parties through the customs that must be upheld. He is a witness to the betrothal transactions, particularly the requisite exchange of bridal gifts and the wedding ceremony. The couple is usually not present during the negotiations.

During this period, the first visit between the families is a get-acquainted visit. The family of the groom—usually a man and several women as negotiators—goes to the bride's family compound and makes small talk while meeting and greeting each family member. They shake everyone's hand. An elder from the bride's family will broach the subject. That spokesperson might say, "We know but we have to ask—what is your mission here?" The groom's family will quote some proverbs, such as "I want to be a slave in your family." The bride's family will offer more proverbs. The two families will then set a date to meet again.

The Rev. Grantson said, "My wife lived a hundred and forty miles from where I am from, and my family—two women and a man—had to come three times. The same people go all the time. It took about six or seven months."

The second component, the "asking," will happen either on the second visit or over the course of subsequent visits. The groom will formally ask the bride's family for her hand. The same delegation will visit again, carrying liquor, which indicates the seriousness of their proposal. The families then haggle over what the young woman will need to start her life with her new husband. Although the bridegroom's family sets the price, the bride's family is free to reject an insufficient payment.

Wrongly called a dowry or bride price, typically the gifts, called *lobola* by the Bantus, *tsir nsa* in Akan, and *mahr* among Muslims, include a token amount of money, gold jewelry, baskets, footwear, and six pieces of fabric for the bride. Some families require seven pieces of fabric, which represent the clans that make up the Akan tribe. Six pieces symbolize double stability, as in a three-stooled pot used for cooking. The financial negotiations are sometimes conducted using sticks or beads to symbolize the money being negotiated. The fathers negotiate until an agreeable amount is reached. All the wedding expenses are paid by the groom's family.

Other gifts are shared by the family members, including fabric for the mother, grandmother, and aunts and gifts of liquor and money for the father and other elders. Many Africans say the bride price was never intended to be a transfer of goods or services in exchange for a wife. Instead, it should be considered a token of appreciation to honor a family's generosity and to acknowledge their loss. But today, some African women, and men, caution that the bride price has led to greed. Many families ask for expensive gifts—new homes, cars, or so much money that it must be paid in installments.

Less wealthy families might give food such as yams or plantains, or cattle or other animals. The families now fix a date for the wedding, which commonly takes place during the third or fourth quarter of the moon or at some other time specified by tradition or religious convention. Easter, Christmas, or at the beginning of a new year

THE GILLMANS
WITH THEIR
TRADITIONAL
BLACK WEDDING
CAKE

are times in which marriages are enacted or engagements are sought.

The third stage, "taking," involves accepting the negotiated articles and the actual marriage. The groom's family may carry the ceremonial payments to the bride's parents in a wooden box or trunk, which starts the ceremony. The couple may have two ceremonies, one a Christian or Muslim ceremony, and another that follows cultural traditions. The formal handing over of the bride takes place at the groom's home.

The bride meanwhile has been bathed and anointed with perfumed oils and dressed in beautiful clothes. On the appointed date, she leaves for the groom's home, escorted by chaperones from her family. Young girls follow with her trousseau—clothing, pots and pans, and household utensils.

At this meeting, the father of the bride might place the couple's hands in the hand of the groom's father, and the groom's father would join their hands together, signifying the intertwining of the families. It also acknowledges that the bride's father has passed the responsibility for his daughter to the father of the groom. This is followed by the couple's declaration of their willingness to be married.

In other instances, according to *Kinship and Marriage Among the Anlo Ewe* by G. K. Nukunya, the chaperone may hand over the bride with these words: "The parents of the bride have given her to us to bring to you in response to your request. From now on, responsibility for her maintenance lies with you. She must be well fed. You must take good care of her when she is sick. We do not quarrel in our house and we do not want her to quarrel in your house."

The groom's father or an elder receives the bride and thanks the chaperones. Both parents give advice. The groom's father might give a speech about the basic necessities of marriage: patience, tolerance, understanding of each other's point of view, and above all, hard work and cooperation in economic and household activities.

The couple's responsibilities to each other are detailed. Then a prayer to the ancestors—a libation—seals the marriage, which is called *ayefor* in Akan, meaning new loins or where the children are.

▶ In some Ghanaian ceremonies, a pastor or elder requests a cup of palm wine. He sips, beckons to the bride to come and sip, then hands the cup to the groom. The groom, meanwhile, is hidden in the crowd of family and friends. The bride searches for him and he is found hiding, crouched down among the crowd.

▶ In some parts of Nigeria and South Africa as well as in other countries, the wedding includes a naming ceremony for the bride and groom to solemnize their new lives together.

► In Nigeria, a family elder might present to their new family members an *ofo*—a short stick from the *Detarium elastica* tree, which is a symbol of unity, truth, and indestructibility.

► Some Nigerian weddings among the Yoruba include a mock bride at the engagement ceremony.

► In some Yoruba ceremonies, the community might use millet instead of rice to be thrown at the bride and groom. Millet represents fertility, children, and wealth.

In Nigeria, they might recite this proverb: "We do not ask for wealth because he that has health and children will also have wealth. We do not pray to have more money but to have more kinsmen. We are better than animals because we have kinsmen. An animal rubs its aching flank against a tree; a man asks his kinsmen to scratch him."

Contemporary African Weddings

Some modern African couples are forgoing some of the traditional rituals. For instance, Siphokazi Koyana, who is South African, married Zola Pinda in a civil ceremony in 1993 in Philadelphia. They had met in South Africa, just as Sipho was about to return to the United States to continue her schooling. They were engaged and left South Africa after a whirlwind courtship. But the last time they went home in January 1996, they tried to pick up on Xhosa traditions they had left behind.

Sipho drew the line, however, at the *lobola,* or bride price, which she said could have been as much as $10,000 for an educated bride with no children. When her mother inquired, Sipho said, "I told her no. He is in school." The tradition used to work well in a more agricultural society, but she feels it has become corrupted. "People ask for ridiculous amounts of money. Some are exchanging their daughters for material gain."

Their first visit home to Ngqushwa, a rural area in the Eastern Cape region, required that they call on both families to apologize for Zola taking his bride without following protocol—the elder men in his family meeting with her parents for premarital discussions. A goat was slaughtered in a naming ceremony. The slaughtering, Sipho says, was the traditional religious part of the ceremony. Instead of a libation with a liquid offering, this ceremony required a blood offering. "The animal's blood is used to communicate with ancestors born in the land," she says. "The blood from the goat must soak into the soil, to evoke ancestors buried in the earth."

Zola's family gave Sipho a new name, Nosango, which means "gatekeeper." The name admonishes her to always keep the gate open for his family. "They gave me that name because when they come to visit they don't want to be afraid to go in." Both families came for the celebration, where she was required to demonstrate the proper virtuous behavior of a bride. Instead of a honeymoon, Xhosa tradition requires that the bride go to the home of the bridegroom's family to show how good a wife she will be, she said. Because she was unable to perform the traditional two-week ceremony after wedding, Sipho spent a day with Zola's family—cooking and cleaning.

During the day she had to wear a traditional costume—a long, heavy cotton three-piece brown-and-white Dutch print dress. Over it, she wore an apron, with a towel wrapped around her middle and a small blanket over her shoulders. On her head, she wore a heavy silk headcloth, over a cotton headcloth to cushion the head for carrying packages.

At another family celebration, her elders gave her advice on how to be a good wife. "Make sure your husband is always full and never hungry. When he comes home late, never ask where he's coming from." Although this is probably not advice she will take, Sipho recognizes its importance.

"We are living between two cultures; you just have to separate the two in your head," said Sipho.

The next time they go home, in 1999, Zola's family will visit Sipho's family. "It's really just a way for the families to meet and get to know each other," she said.

Many other transplanted Africans are returning to familiar family traditions to find a mate.

After living many years abroad, an Egyptian man returned to his home in 1994 to find a wife. His family began the search and mentioned a suitable young woman. When he arrived home, his brother made arrangements for them to meet at her parents' home. With their talk began their formal engagement. He spent several weeks getting to know her and her family. He traveled to visit her nearly every day. With her family, he discussed the gift he would give his fiancée and how much he would spend on it. He bought her a gold necklace and gold wedding rings for them both as a sign of his serious intentions. He wore his wedding band on his right hand until the wedding ceremony, when he transferred it to the left.

After the engagement, everybody in the town was invited to have sweets, cakes, or sodas at celebrations in the homes of the family members of the bride and groom.

A Muslim wedding ceremony was held, and family and friends were again invited. A judge gave the declaration of marriage. He sat between the couple, covered their hands with cloth, and recited the words of marriage: "In the name of God, we witness that this man is the husband of this woman." In a third celebration, the guests went from house to house in celebration. Women started singing with

SIPHOKAZI KOYANA (RIGHT) AND HER RELATIVES DRESS IN TRADITIONAL SOUTH AFRICAN OUTFITS FOR A WEDDING RITUAL IN WHICH SIPHO ATTENDS HER HUSBAND'S FAMILY.

happiness. There were dancers, singers, and music from noon until nearly ten in the evening. Then the bride moved into her husband's home.

Free to Marry

BROOMSTICK WEDDINGS

In the antebellum period in the United States, marriages were celebrated and protected by law, except for those of slaves. As legal chattel, most were not allowed this sanctioning in a court or a church. By the late 18th century, religious groups began to lobby for slave masters to allow their slaves to marry. Later some plantation owners supervised such unions, hoping that the marriages would enforce a social control that would deter slave rebellion and runaways.

Although many slaves lived for years as common-law husband and wife without any ceremony, they longed for the rites of passage many of us today take for granted. Still many others pursued the quest for legitimacy in such ceremonies as jumping the broom or crossing sticks, in ribbon-tying ceremonies or in weddings in blankets, before they returned to their often separate plantations. Jumping the broom was certainly the most common ritual to celebrate slave couples' quest for validation and meaning.

For them, the broomstick or other ritual served the same purpose as a sanctioned ceremony: It elevated their relationship to a legitimate union and signified their passage into adulthood. It also signaled their acceptance of new obligations and responsibilities to their families and their community.

However, slaves were not the only people to jump the broom. Historians record similar ceremonies among poor whites in the South as well as among itinerant laborers in New England and even among some Gypsies. It was once even accepted as common-law marriage among whites by local authorities.

Slave narratives compiled by the 1930s Works Projects Administration recorded the thoughts and recollections of many elderly ex-slaves about the rite of marriage. Some women told of their brutalized lives and of being forced by their masters or other slaves to marry men not of their choosing. The men had similar recollections. They were forced to take up with women they didn't love and didn't want. Many had no ceremonies; they said if they wanted to be married and the master agreed, they were married. Others told of ceremonies in the field between rows that they themselves had plowed. Still others told of being married in blankets; they just moved their blanket into the next cabin where their love interest lived.

However, many slaves were angry at their inability to wed legally. Their unstable status provoked this bitter benediction from one black preacher: "Now before God and witnesses, I pronounce you man and wife. And whomsoever God has solated to be joined together, let no man part asunder. Cursed is he that part man and wife. Amen."

Still others told stories of true love and blissful relations. Some plantations prepared for slave weddings almost like a party, with full tables, decorations, fancy attire, musicians, dancing, and gaiety. Many of these events were for the slave master's entertainment. For the slave couple, it was an opportunity to celebrate.

Charlotte Beverly of Texas recalled her 19th-century wedding: "When I marry my sister marry too and our husbands was brothers. My husband dress in suit of white linen. He sho look handsome. He give me a gold ring and a cup and saucer for a weddin gift. We git married in Huntsville and us didnt go on a weddin journey trip. We was so poor we couldn go round the house."*

Similarly, Phoebe Henderson, also of Texas, demonstrates that love can find its way even under the most dire circumstances. "My husband's name was David Henderson and we lived on the same plantation and belonged to the same man. No sir, Master Hill

*From *American Slave: A Composite Autobiography*, George P. Rawick, ed., suppl. series (Westport, Conn.: Greenwood Publishing Co., 1979).

didn't have nothin to do with bringin us together. I guess God done it. We fell in love and David asked Master Hill for me. We had a weddin in the house, was married by a colored Baptist preacher. I wore a white cotton dress and Missus Hill give me a pan of flour for a weddin present. He give us a house of our own. My husband was good to me. He was a careful man and not rowdy. When we'd go anywhere, we'd ride horseback and I'd ride behin him."*

And Harriet Jones married her husband, Bill, a year after freedom. Whites and blacks gathered in the moonlight under a big elm tree. She had two flower girls to hold her train. She wore a dress borrowed from her mistress, red stockings, new shoes, and a wide-brimmed hat. She recalled the preacher's words:

> *Dark and stormy may come the weather,*
> *I jines dis man and woman together.*
> *Let none but Him what makes de thunder*
> *Put dis man and woman asunder.*

The reception was held in the backyard. The food was set on a table made from two planks and decorated with a white tablecloth, red berries, and red candles. They dined on barbecued pig, roasted sweet potatoes, dumplings, pies, and cakes. The celebration continued at a neighbor's: "Den we goes to Marse Watson's saddle shop to dance and dances all night and de bride and groom, dat's us, leads de grand march."†

After Emancipation

When freedmen and women were allowed to sanctify their unions, Freedman Bureau records showed thousands did so with great enthusiasm despite many hardships. Some even married more than once to be sure it had been done correctly. Many municipalities

---

*From *American Slave: A Composite Autobiography,* George P. Rawick, ed.

†From *The Black Family in Slavery and Freedom: 1750–1925* by Herbert G. Gutman (New York: Pantheon Books, 1976).

In Belize, the wedding walk is a bride's last stroll as a single woman. As she makes her way to the church, people in the town throw gifts and compliment her on how beautiful she looks.

In Haiti, a community wedding celebration is often accompanied by voodoo songs for the occasion.

charged a small fee to register the marriages of ex-slaves. For many of the impoverished freedmen and women, that fee was a burden they were more than willing to bear. They scrimped and saved for the needed twenty-five cents or more. They industriously sold wares or produce, or bartered for the needed funds to register their marriages.

In Muhlenberg, Kentucky, a marriage book recorded black marriages starting in April 1866, shortly after a law was passed freeing slaves in the state and legalizing marriages between blacks and mulattoes as well. The law read:

SECTION 1: That all negroes and mulattoes may inter-marry with each other in the same manner and under the same regulations that are provided by law for white persons: Provided, that the clerk of the county court shall keep separate records of the same. In addition to the persons now authorized by law to solemnize marriage, marriages between negroes and mulattoes may be solemnized by any minister in good standing of any recognized church of colored persons.

SECTION 2: All negroes and mulattoes who have heretofore lived and cohabited and do now live together as husband and wife, shall be taken and held in law as legally married and the issue held as legitimate for all purposes: Provided such persons shall appear before the clerk of the county court of their then residence, and declare that they have been and desire to continue living together as husband and wife, when, upon the receipt of a fee of fifty cents, the clerk shall make a record of such declaration and for an additional fee of twenty-five cents, shall furnish the parties with a certificate of said declaration. Said record or certificate shall be evidence of the existence of the marriage and the legitimacy of the issue to said parties, provided, the issue or customary marriages of negroes shall be held legitimate.

This marriage affidavit was certified in Kentucky.

> This is to certify that on the 10th day of March 1866 the rites of marriage were legally solemnized by me between Marion Green and Hannah Weir at the African Church in Greenville, in the county of Muhlenberg, in the presence of Robert Metcalf, Charles Jones. Signed: Samuel Elliot, Pastor.

MODERN ADAPTATIONS

Despite the terribly painful memories of slavery, some couples have decided to embrace their history rather than reject it. At the Imperial Broom Company, the Robinson family has been making and selling ceremonial brooms for nearly ninety years. Owner Matthew Robinson says he makes hundreds of brooms a year for couples seeking the ceremony. Even more, couples from all ethnic backgrounds are seeking brooms as an important folk symbol of marriage. He says in the past ten years, many Jewish couples have asked him to make brooms tied with a bag of sugar—to ensure a clean, sweet marriage. Others are seeking rough, raw brooms made the old-fashioned way. His staff creates them from saplings, by gathering a coarse bunch of straws and stitching them onto the sapling broomstick.

Some folklorists feel these rituals may have an African link. Other historians say such rituals are illegitimate and are an insult to African culture and a debasement of the sanctity of marriage. And some elders from the islands of Trinidad and Tobago tell of couples who jumped the broom in the old days, before the book or movie *Roots*.

But others say it is simply an act of remembrance so couples never forget the struggles of our past that have made us the strong, resilient people we are today.

The Rev. Patrick Keen, a Chicagoan who had a second wedding complete with African rituals and broom jumping, said he attended a seminar in which ministers from other cultures spoke about using symbolism to enhance ceremonies. "What we lifted up was pulling out from your culture the nuances. The same thing must happen for us. We can celebrate our western culture and we can do that from our African heritage. I am called to help African Americans in the Lutheran church find how do we celebrate within the confines of eurocentric culture."

Rev. Grantson says the broom holds significance for African cultures. He says broom jumping was an innovation that was informed by the culture. Among the Akan of Ghana, the broom symbolizes hearth, family, cleanliness.

Rabbi Capers C. Funnye Jr. of Chicago says consider the legacy of jumping the broom as a leap of faith on the part of our ancestors. Repeating this poignant ritual offers important instruction for life: "When you are apt to forget it, you are apt to repeat it."

Los Angeles actress Monique Ridge decided that she would marry Otis Williams in a reproduction of a slave ceremony on a 19th-century plantation in Plano, Texas, outside Dallas. She took the story of Tempie Durham from slave narratives and created a script for the wedding. The era of slavery holds an intense fascination for Monique. She wanted to authenticate the period in food, fashion, and ceremony. His suit was made of raw silk to simulate the burlap or croker sack from which slave clothing was often made. And she wore a dress similarly worn during the 19th century made from three styles of silk. A dancer carried an umbrella covered with corn to symbolize fertility. A nine-member a capella chorus sang slave hymns. The mood was ethereal.

"I knew it couldn't be like it was, so I made a slice of what it could have been. I didn't want younger people to feel there was anything shameful about having been a slave. There was still a celebration of life. A celebration of existence."

The invitation featured a picture of the barn on the plantation. The programs were printed on church fans. The food consisted of Southern fare with place settings that included mason jars on tables covered by muslin and burlap and tubs of homemade lemonade. The couple relied on the preacher to offer the vows as once done in slavery times. And together, they jumped the broom.

Jumping the Broom

It is no coincidence that we are never at a loss for words at a wedding. Years of tradition and adherence to ritual have given ministers, spiritual leaders, and other officiants a repertoire of tried and true ceremonies that many couples recite without a second thought. Some people are grateful for an elder who can lead them step by step through a period of immense emotional upheaval. But others would rather use their wedding as an opportunity to reflect and savor the moment that they cross over a new threshold in life. The ceremonies and vows given here are intended to offer those people an understanding of how to find more personal words to grace their ceremony. Although the vows may be used verbatim, they serve only to guide couples to create their own special moments.

A reprint of vows created by one couple from a ceremony in the 1970s demonstrates a concern for integrating the modern with the past, the individual with the community. It echoes the sentiments of Kwanzaa, and offers couples a means to blend African tradition with modern African-American sensibilities.

There is a ceremony in which the Nguzo Saba, or seven important principles to live by—unity, self-determination, collective responsibility, cooperative economics, purpose, creativity, and faith —are incorporated into wedding vows.

There is a ceremony that utilizes Yoruba philosophies, such as the tasting of kola nut, a source of strength; honey to add sweetness; water to freshen; or pepper to test a groom's strength.

There are vows that can be incorporated into a wedding ceremony. There is also a slave ceremony to give the reader the historical and cultural significance of the ritual, as well as a poem that can be used by those who want something appropriate to be said as they jump the broom.

A Wedding Assembly

For slaves, wedding ceremonies were often dictated by their labors. Multiple weddings were common during Christmas holidays when chores abated and households planned for holiday celebrations. The weddings were usually conducted by self-proclaimed black preachers, spiritual leaders, or male or female plantation elders. They quoted Scriptures they had learned or memorized because many couldn't read.

Slaves were quite aware that the laws denied them an essential right by not sanctioning their marriages. So among themselves, they accorded their weddings the solemnity and sanctity they felt due in their broomstick ceremonies. One Virginia freedwoman acknowledged a bitter truth: "God made marriage but the white man made the law."

This ceremony was held in 1856 for several couples. The master led the ceremonies on a Saturday night.

We are assembled together tonight on an occasion of much interest. It is a marriage occasion, but it is of a novel

SHIRLEY
WILLIAMS
KIRKSEY AND
GARY KIRKSEY
JUMPED THE
BROOM AT THEIR
WEST VIRGINIA
WEDDING.

and peculiar character. It is not the ordinary occasion of one couple of persons, but the very unusual one—perhaps unprecedented one, of the marriage at the same time with the same ceremony, of seven separate couples. The parties who are to be married now stand in a circle before us, each couple hand in hand. The couples are Alfred and Ermine, Isaac and Rosa, Bennett and Catherine, Allen and Harriet, Ben and Emma, Lewis and Peggy, and Horace and Betty.

The vows were repeated to each couple.

Alfred, do you agree before me and these witnesses to take Ermine as your wife and to solemnly pledge yourself to discharge towards him the duties of an affectionate and faithful husband?

I do.

Ermine, do you agree before me and these witnesses to take Alfred as your husband and to solemnly pledge yourself to discharge towards him the duties of an affectionate and faithful wife?

I do.

We have now gone through with every form necessary to authorize me to pronounce each of these several couples as man and wife. We have heard each party, of each couple, agree to enter into the married relation with the other party; and we have heard from each to the other a solemn vow of fidelity to the obligations of the married state. It only remains, therefore, that I should pronounce and accordingly, in the presence of these witnesses, I do pronounce Alfred and Ermine, Isaac and Rosa, Bennett and Catherine, Allen and Harriet, Ben and Emma, Lewis and Peggy, and Horace and Betty as man and wife. And in conclusion, I enjoin, according to the good old customs of our fathers and mothers, that each bridegroom now salute the bride.

A Yoruba Wedding

A wedding in the tradition of Yoruba begins with a spiritual reading before the wedding by a *babalawo* or high priest. The reading determines whether the future surrounding the couple is in harmony. It also advises them how to eliminate all possible negatives to ensure harmony for their marriage. Sometimes an *ebo,* an offering, is made to Osun—the governing *orisha* or spirit of love, money, and conception—before the wedding ceremony to rid the couple of family conflicts. Sometimes marriages are governed by the orisha Obatala, who offers calmness, tranquility, wisdom, and tolerance to set the tone for the wedding. The spiritual reading should be done at least a month before the wedding to help draw a more positive vibration for the nuptials. The officiant throws a kola nut to divine whether the ancestors bless the union. If not, the babalawo will suggest an offering by lighting a candle or other rituals.

At the ceremony, an altar is filled with baskets of food and fruit to welcome the ancestors. The groom's family and his groomsmen place the food at the altar. The delicacies might include honey, pumpkin, or yams as a gift to Osun. This ceremony is adapted from one performed by Babalawo Ade Ifaleri Olayinka.

POURING THE LIBATION

A wedding, like all important events in African society, starts with the pouring of a libation. An essential part of any ritual, a libation is simply a prayer accompanied by an offering. It uses water, or more often liquor, which is poured on the ground after each entreaty. If it cannot be poured directly on the ground, it is collected and taken outside and later poured into the earth, the resting place for ancestors. The libation calls upon and asks blessings from God, ancestral spirits, then the living dead—those family members who have recently passed on. An officiant will call the names of the couple's ancestors who have died as well as calling the name of the bride and groom.

A babalawo or family elder might say:

> *God of the crossroads, open a path to fresh water,*
> *Freshen the road that our ancestors must travel to*
> *   be here.*
> *Cleanse the house from all that is evil,*
> *Cleanse the house from all sickness,*
> *Cleanse the house from all tragedy.*

We pray to the Creator for calmness, coolness.
We pray to the mothers and fathers of all our
    ancestors.
We pray for prosperity.
We pray that Gyasi and Imani's faith will always
    be strong.
We pray that they trust each other.
We pray that they will always honor the truth.
May death be no more,
May loss be no more,
May tragedy be no more,
May disease be no more,
May nothing be overwhelming.
Ashe.

The groom, his groomsmen, parents of the bride, and family elders enter and stand at the front before the altar.

The bride and her escorts—friends and relatives—circle the room three times before she is presented to the groom. As he lifts her long veil, he registers shock that it is the wrong woman, a mock bride. The surprise offers a moment of levity, and tests the groom to see if he is certain about the woman he wants.

The bride enters, escorted by her bridesmaids, and stands next to the groom.

Groom: (To the mother of the bride.) May I have your blessing to marry your daughter?

Mother: Yes. But I have several questions for you. Do you trust in God with all your heart? Will you let Him direct your path? Will you love, cherish, and support my daughter, and listen with your heart?

Groom: Yes, I will.

Congregation: Ashe (amen).

Symbolic presenting of the *lobola*. The groom presents gifts to the bride's family that symbolize his ability to care for his wife and his thanks to the family for having taken good care of her. Gifts may include jewelry, fertility symbols, and various household items.

Babalawo: Now the groom and bride will speak of their feelings for each other.

Groom: When I met Imani, I was amazed by her spirit. Not only is she a beautiful woman but she is an honorable and spiritual woman. Since I met her, my life has been enriched and my heart full of love for her.

Bride: Since I met Gyasi, I found a soul mate. He is attentive to my every need. He is an honorable man and he has shown his love for me in so many ways.

Babalawo: Father, mother, by accepting these gifts you acknowledge Gyasi's honorable intentions to care for your daughter and you signal your permission for your daughter to marry.

Bride's father: I accept.

Groom's father: Gyasi and Imani have our blessing.

TASTING THE SPICES

Babalawo: Taste is an essential sense. Just one taste can bring back a flood of memories. Even without sight, we know what we have if we can just taste it. It is the same for Afoshe—this ceremony of the tasting of the spices.

Every time you taste these spices, you will remember this moment. And during times when you forget why you are still together, it will remind you of the loving emotions you originally had for each other. First the groom, then the bride, will taste the spices, then it will be passed to the parents, family, and members of the community as a sign of our ties to one another.

Taste of this kola nut. It is a sacred spice used for divination. In Egypt, it was used to call upon the spirits. We use this bitter herb today as a symbol of the bitterness that life can bring. We pray this element helps you to be wise to sidestep those bitter lessons. To give you the knowledge to solve your problems. To help you incorporate life's experience in your everyday survival. We pray that you pass your knowledge on to your children.

Water represents the abundance of life and the blessings of life. No life can exist without water. It is everywhere within us, covering the lands. It quenches our thirst; it refreshes our bodies; it cleanses, it's sacred, it's vital. It represents the spirit of Osun—the ancestral body governing marriage, prosperity, children, love, happiness. May life's waters flood your home with an abundance of happiness, health, and wealth.

Honey brings sweetness into the home. This taste is to help the sweetness in your marriage continue to spread. Remember to treat each other with respect and love and to always have sweet words for one another.

Pepper is for the spice of life. We all experience hot things, the trials and tribulations of life. May you have enough pepper to keep your marriage spicy but not so much that the passion singes your love and creates jealousy or anger.

Salt is an all-purpose spice. Our ancestors were enslaved because of the pursuit of salt. It was first used in Mali as a preservative. But it also adds flavor. May this taste of salt help preserve all that is good in your marriage.

EXCHANGING RINGS

> *Officiant:* We are standing on the shoulders of our
> ancestors.
>
> *Community:* Ashe.
>
> *Officiant:* Trust in God and he will not forsake you.
> Grow happy. Respect each other.

The officiant brings out two white doves as a symbol of love and happiness.

> *Officiant:* These doves represent purity, harmony,
> peace, and we release them to give it back to the
> world.

He touches the couple with the doves, which are then released into the sky.

Kwanzaa Ceremony

This ceremony combines the seven principles of Kwanzaa. It is appropriate for a wedding in December, when the holiday is celebrated, or it can be used at any other time of year.

> *Officiant:* Dear hearts, we have gathered on this joyous
> occasion to welcome Gyasi and Imani over the
> threshold into holy matrimony. It is not an occasion
> to be taken lightly. Marriage confirms our family cus-
> toms. It is a spiritual rite of passage that links us to
> our spiritual ancestors—the source of life. And it
> joins us with our descendants—those to whom we
> give life. It is a celebration that magnifies our success-
> ful quest to form a spiritual bond. It cements families,
> builds nations, and strengthens the community.

We have come as family, friends, and community to witness this blessed union. By our presence, we wish to demonstrate our love and support for this couple. By our presence, we promise to help shoulder the troubles in times of tribulation and to rejoice with them in times of celebration.

We call on God, Creator of heaven and earth and sustainer of all life, to bear witness to this blessed occasion. We ask that you keep Gyasi and Imani in the palm of your powerful hands. We ask you to stand guard against all who would mean them and theirs ill will. Give them the strength of our slave ancestors to endure and overcome all of life's trials and tribulations. Give them the wisdom of our African ancestors to guide them through life's harsh terrain. We ask that you to smile down upon them and make their lives fruitful with children and with love. Grant them bountiful harvests in the field, respect in their community, and serenity at home.

On their part, Gyasi and Imani have committed to uphold the Nguzo Saba, the seven principles of Kwanzaa. These seven principles—*umoja,* unity; *kujichagulia,* self-determination; *ujima,* collective responsibility; *ujamaa,* cooperative economics; *nia,* purpose; *kuumba,* creativity; and *imani,* faith—offer instructive guidelines for marriage and for life. We know that marriage offers joy as well as sorrow. We know that companionship can breed love as well as hate. But we also know that with God's guidance, all life's worries can be overcome.

So, Gyasi, in the presence of God and community, what are your intentions?

Groom: My intentions are to offer Imani a husband who is faithful, strong, and kind. I promise to love and

honor her. I promise to make patience, understanding, and cooperation a cornerstone of our lives
together. I promise to uphold my love in sickness
and health, in poverty and wealth. This I promise
from now until forever.

So, Imani, in the presence of God and community, what
are your intentions?

Bride: My intentions are to offer Gyasi a wife who is
faithful and kind. I promise to love and honor him.
I promise to make patience, understanding, and
cooperation a cornerstone of our lives together. I
promise to uphold my love in sickness and health, in
poverty and wealth. This I promise from now until
forever.

LIGHTING CANDLES

Next comes the lighting of the seven candles of Kwanzaa. The bride
and groom start on opposite ends and join in the middle.

Groom: I light this candle to signify *umoja*—unity. We
join our our lives together and link our destiny to
that of our ancestors. May we learn to use the wisdom of our elders to guide us through life's ups and
downs.

Bride: I light this candle to signify *kujichagulia*—self-
determination—so that we may freely determine the
right path for us and our family.

Groom: I light this candle to signify *ujima*—collective
responsibility. Together we work to elevate our family and our community.

Bride: I light this candle to signify *ujamaa*—cooperative economics. Together we will work to make our
family and community economically viable.

Groom: I light this candle to signify *nia*, or purpose.

Together we will make the purpose of our words evident by our good deeds.

Bride: I light this candle to signify *kuumba*—creativity. We will support creative endeavors and life-affirming changes.

Together: We light this candle to signify *imani*, or faith. It is faith that has brought us this far, and we continue to believe that like our ancestors, we will march toward a life that offers freedom, honor, and respect.

EXCHANGING RINGS

Officiant: These rings represent life's eternity. And you give these as a symbol of your spiritual bond. May your love follow life's course, never yielding in times of sorrow and always strengthening in times of joy. Let them be a sign of a love that knows no bounds.

Groom: I give this ring as a token of my abiding love for you. With it, I promise to uphold you as my eternal companion. And I promise to treasure it and our lives together.

Bride: I give this ring as a token of my abiding love for you. With it, I promise to uphold you as my eternal companion. And I promise to treasure it and our lives together.

Officiant: Eternal God, giver of life, grant Gyasi and Imani the strength to weather any storm. Give them the tools to build monuments to their love. Give them the generosity to share their fortunes. And give them the wisdom to lead their families to victory. Anoint their household with honey to sweeten the bitterness in life. Let them not shrink from the taste of pepper so they may shoulder the burdens in life. Purify their home with clear water to freshen the

path to your wisdom, and give them the resolve to
turn evil away from their door.

May you live in joy. I now pronounce you husband and
wife. You may salute your bride.

A Ceremony of Renewal

More and more people are renewing their weddings vows. They do
it to reaffirm their marriage relationship and to remind each other
and their families that their commitment is still solid. It celebrates
the triumph over adversity and the spirit of love, honor, and
respect.

Officiant: When love is sparked, it's an event to be celebrated. When love grows, it's an occasion to rejoice.
When love endures, it's an opportunity to reflect. So
today we pause to honor the sanctity of matrimony.
And to rejoice with two who have found their way
through life's poverty and riches to come before us
to testify that their love has been strengthened, not
weakened, by life's challenges. We have come to bear
witness that with God, devotion can stand the test of
time. Their steadfastness reveals how life's trials and
tribulations have given them many gifts—understanding, patience, wisdom, forbearance, and mercy.
They want to testify that life's bounty has gifted
them with generosity, grace, and charity. You have
been invited to take part in a celebration of renewal.
This couple would like to reaffirm the vows they
made to each other many years ago. They knew little
then about the path their relationship would take.
They could not know what the grab bag we call life
would hold for them. They knew little of what to

expect from each other. Their lives were an empty slate, untried and unproven. But they stand before you today—yes—tested, tried, and true. They want you to know that it was not always easy. They don't claim to be free from mistakes and misunderstandings. But they recognize the secret to their success is that they are always slow to anger and quick to make amends. Let us pray.

THE INVOCATION

Officiant: Father God, look down upon your children. They have come to say thank you for years of happiness. They have come to make a testimony about what devotion can do. They ask that you be with them here today in the presence of their children, their friends and family. They ask that you gather everyone here in the safety of your sheltering arms. They ask that you spread the blessings they have received from your care. Father God, allow them to use their love's longevity to sow hope that others can find their way to a long-lasting marriage. Father God, allow others to see in them the prescription for a resilient union. All this we ask in your name. Amen.

THE EXPRESSION OF INTENT

Officiant: You have already proven your steadfastness and devotion. You have already proven your ability to raise strong, healthy children. We know that you have consoled each other in sickness and have enjoyed each other in health. We know you have weathered times of poverty and rejoiced in times of prosperity. So we come today to hear you reaffirm your love and dedication to each other.

Groom:

In the name of God and with a grateful heart,

I, Gyasi, reaffirm my promise I made to you many years
ago.

I promise to continue to love you and honor you,

For better and for worse,

Even in sickness and in health,

For all the days of our lives.

This is my solemn vow.

Bride:

In the name of God and with a grateful heart,

I, Imani, reaffirm my promise I made to you many years
ago.

I promise to continue to love you and honor you,

For better and for worse,

Even in sickness and in health,

For all the days of our lives.

This is my solemn vow.

THE EXCHANGE OF GIFTS

Officiant: What gifts do you share as a token of your
love?

The bride and groom present gifts (which can be related to their
anniversary).

Officiant: Eternal God, who gave us the gift of marriage as a sign of love between man and woman, Gyasi
and Imani exchange these rings as a sign of their abiding love for each other. May they also be signs of
promises fulfilled and unending devotion. Amen.

Groom: I give this gift as a symbol of our covenant, that
all that I have and all that I am, I honor you in the
name of God.

Bride: I give this gift as a symbol of our covenant, that all that I have and all that I am, I honor you in the name of God.

Officiant: Eternal God, creator and preserver of life, author of salvation and giver of grace, bless Gyasi and Imani on the anniversary of their marriage. As you blessed their young lives together, we ask that you continue to bestow your kind blessings upon them. Renew their bounties of joy and peace. May your spirit strengthen them and grant them everlasting love. Allow them to remain steadfast in the service of your work. May the Lord bless you and keep you and may the Lord make His face to shine upon you and give you peace. Amen.

A Ceremony for a Second Marriage

This ceremony encompasses traditions of Africa and America. It seeks to blend families for people who are wedding for a second time. It also blends customs by using African proverbs, which are very much part of the marriage ritual, as well as a broom-jumping segment.

Music is played on drums and on the *kalimba,* or thumb piano. The groom and groomsmen dance in. The groom walks down the aisle with his children. They sit in the front pew. The bride enters with her children. They also sit in the front pew.

The officiant starts the ceremony with a libation.

Officiant: Greetings in the name of God and our ancestors. When I say "Agoo," feel free to answer with "Ameh," which signifies your agreement to what I am saying.

We call on the spirit of the Creator and the spirit of our

ancestors to rid this place of all who would wish harm to this man and woman. Use your spirit to guide the ceremony and again to rid the evil that may be present in the room and to alter the ill will of anyone who came to bestow anything other than good wishes. Agoo.

Congregation: Ameh.

Officiant: All marriages are occasions to rejoice but doubly so in a second marriage. You have healed from the pain of a wounded heart and have weathered the cold winds of loneliness. Love has left you bruised but not broken. Suffering, as they say, makes you stronger. And with this strength, you understand better the frailties of human spirit. You are older and wiser and assuredly more tolerant. By seeking to marry each other, you have decided that life is better lived not alone but with family. Someone to share the small victories and the large defeats. In Africa, marriage is the essence of family life. A wedding is viewed as a melding of families rather than individuals. And as this is a second marriage, you have more family than before. You have brought children with you into this marriage. Treat them equally. Remember that children are an important part of the family. Nigerians say children give glory to a home. He who has children has many blessings. It is in children that we reveal our legacy. Our children will be here to speak our name when we have long left this earth. With love and understanding, you can make this enlarged unit a source of strength and continuity.

Let us pray.

Our Father, help us to welcome all the newcomers to this family. Bind these once-separate family members into a single loving and secure home. Help them find peace and acceptance among one another. Help them learn to turn to one another for guidance and support. Help them to be tolerant of their differences and to rejoice in their commonalities. Let them come to understand the blessings of family. This we ask in your name's sake. Amen.

THE EXPRESSION OF INTENT

Officiant: Having come to each other older but wiser, Gyasi, do you choose Imani to love and be loved, to cherish and be cherished, in sickness and in health, all the days of your lives?

Groom: I do.

Officiant: And Gyasi, do you declare that with this marriage you will accept responsibility for her children as you would your own? To bind them to you and work to build a strong foundation of love, honor, and respect?

Groom: I do.

Officiant: Having come to each other older but wiser, Imani, do you choose Gyasi to love and be loved, to cherish and be cherished, in sickness and in health, all the days of your lives?

Bride: I do.

Officiant: And Imani, do you declare that with this marriage you will accept responsibility for his children as you would your own? To bind them to you and work to build a strong foundation of love, honor, and respect?

Bride: I do.

THE VOWS

Groom: Beloved, I choose you in the sight of God and our families to be my wife. I promise my love will be steadfast. I promise you my tender ministrations during sickness and in health. I promise to support you and protect you and defend you from life's harsh blows. Your family shall be my family, and together we shall benefit from this call to unity.

Bride: Beloved, I choose you in the sight of God and our families to be my husband. I promise my love will be steadfast. I promise you my tender ministrations during sickness and in health. I promise to support you and protect you and defend you from life's harsh blows. Your family shall be my family, and together we shall benefit from this call to unity.

EXCHANGING THE RINGS

Groom: Take this ring as a symbol of my sweet embrace. Accept it as a constant reminder that I will always honor and uphold our covenant of love.

THE PRONOUNCEMENT OF MARRIAGE

Officiant: With the merging of these two hearts comes the joining of two families. The saying goes that the ties established between two families by a happy marriage are stronger than those of wealth. Marriage is not just a religious institution, it is a social institution. Merging two families gives children stability and parameters. It undergirds the community to make it stronger and more durable.

Kente cloth is now presented.

Officiant: Wearing of this kente cloth is wearing a spiritual item made from labors of the Akan people in Ghana. The Akan are master craftsmen. Their products include gold, silver, and kente woven fabrics.

They so value their work that they give names to the patterns in the fabrics that they weave. This one is called "Family Is a Crowd." We wrap the newly joined family in this kente cloth as a symbol of the blending of two families. It signifies the transformation, just as a caterpillar would weave a cocoon and emerges as a butterfly. May this family emerge from its newfound relationship to soar to even greater heights.

Next we ask the elders to come to tie the knot.

The parents and grandparents tie a knot in a strip of kente cloth or the minister's belt.

Officiant: These knots represent the support of the community for this union. As was done by the our slave parents, we tie this knot to tightly bind this family. Each knot represents the work we vow to undertake to keep the family together. It is a symbol of the support of the community and of our family.

Before the wedding
or reception starts,
a woman designated
as the broom mis-
tress can pass out
ribbons to each
guest so they can
write a note of good
wishes to the bride
and groom. The
mistress collects the
ribbons and ties
them on the broom
before the jumping.
The broom may be
placed on the floor
and may simply be
stepped over.

Broom Jumping

The broom mistress brings out the broom, decorated with ribbons.

א *Officiant:* When our people were slaves, the rites of
marriage were forbidden to us. For them, jumping
the broom became the ritual by which they pursued
the passage of marriage. The slaves remembered the
act but not the meaning behind the act. The broom
is a household symbol in many parts of Africa. For
instance, the Akan use brooms to sweep away evil.
They sweep their homes to rid them of any evil lurk-
ing in the corners. Today that broom stands as a
symbol of the ingenuity and the devotion by which
our ancestors re-created a solemn rite under adverse
conditions. As many a slave ancestor recited: Jump
high, jump wide, the first to touch the broom is the
first to die.*

These words are also appropriate for those who want to include
a broom jumping as part of their wedding celebration. I created
them to be recited by a broom mistress just before the jumping
takes place, after the wedding or at the reception.

> *Dear God above, unite these young lovers.*
> *May their paths lead them always to one another.*
> *They vow to heed our culture's past.*
> *And give to the future—may their love long last.*
> *Rejoice, reclaim, tell everyone your name;*
> *Tell your children and their children*
> *Of the history you claim.*

---

*Adapted from a ceremony by the Reverend Emmanuel F. Y. Grantson.

We knot these broom ribbons as a symbol of
The ties that bind these two families in love.
Two hearts, one love—this bride and groom
Unite in marriage by jumping the broom.

An Afrikan Wedding

Ann and Chester Grundy wrote the vows for their 1974 wedding. They researched African traditions and incorporated cultural aspects from several countries. At the time, it represented a groundbreaking change in the way black marriages were conducted. They were proud to lead the way.

All praises be to our creator.

All praises be to black people.

All praises be to our ancestors who have brought us to this point.

All praises be to our children who are our hope for tomorrow.

All praises be to all who have gathered here today to join these two people and these two families.

Just as marriage symbolizes a decision by two people to come together as one, so the wedding ceremony itself represents the manner in which those two people will approach the world.

We are an Afrikan people and even though we are far from the loving shores of our Motherland, Afrika still speaks to us. An Afrikan wedding symbolizes a bond which has not and cannot be broken. An Afrikan wedding ceremony speaks to us of seven principles—the Nguzo Saba—which are the foundation of an Afrikan family life.

These principles are: *Umoja*—unity. To strive for and maintain unity in our community, nation, and race.

Kujichagulia—self-determination. To define ourselves and speak for ourselves instead of being defined and spoken for by others. *Ujima*—collective work and responsibility. To build and maintain our community together and to make our brothers' and sisters' problems our problems and to solve them together. *Ujamaa*—cooperative economics. To build and maintain our own shops and other businesses and to profit together from them. *Nia*—purpose. To make our collective vocation the building and developing of our community in order to restore our people to their traditional greatness. *Kuumba*—creativity. To always do as much as we can in the way we can in order to leave our community more beautiful and beneficial than when we inherited it. *Imani*—faith. To believe with all our hearts in our parents, our teachers, our leaders, our people, and the righteousness and the victory of our struggle.

THE DRINKING OF THE WINE

Officiant: We share this wine in the spirit of the timeless tradition of our common Mother Afrika. With this act, we shall unite these two families, for that which binds these two people shall also bind these two houses.

The wine vessel is passed to all participating family members. Then the ceremony continues with the exchanging of vows.

THE VOWS

Abdul Akbar's vows:
I have chosen you, Bandele, to walk through this life
    with me;
To be my companion,
The mother of my children, and

The object of my love.
Your struggles shall be our struggles
And your happiness will be our happiness.
To you, I promise:
The devotion of my heart,
The protection of my house,
And the strength and light of the Nguzo Saba.

Bandele's vows:

I love you, Abdul, and want to build my life with you
    because I have seen in you the very best in our race.
I love you because you believe in the principles of the
    Nguzo Saba.
I love you because you take seriously the business of
    nation building.
I love you because you take seriously my womanhood
    and my Afrikanness, which are one and the same.
I love you because I want more than all else to share
    with you in the struggles of our people.
And most of all, I love you for what I am when I am
    with you.
It is my desire, Abdul, to be your wife.

A libation is poured.

Never at a Loss for Words

The Rev. Emmanuel F. Y. Grantson created this wedding vow in which the groom puts his right hand on the bride's shoulders as they face each other. He said this gesture is used to get the attention of the guests, but also symbolizes the responsibility for each other that both accept as husband and wife. The groom repeats the vows after the pastor. Then the bride does the same.

Groom: I, Gyasi, put my hand on you this day. I open
my mouth and declare before God, my ancestors,
and this congregation: I take you, Imani, to be my
wife. I love you and will make you mine. In bitter
days and days of sweetness, in darkness and in light,
in death and in life, I will walk in step with you.
Your matters will be my matters. Think about me the
way I think about you. And together we will triumph
in our struggles. I will be with you all the days of my
life. This is my vow. I have spoken.

AFROCENTRIC VOWS

These vows were created by wedding consultant Deborah Lewis-
Kearns as a result of many requests from couples who were seeking
an alternative to the traditional wedding vows. It is appropriate for
any wedding. The bride and groom may personalize it by inserting
their names.

Bride:
Before this assembly of family and friends,
I pledge my love for you,
A love as deep as the rivers of our native continent,
As strong as our people,
And as enduring as our legacy of faith.
I pray that the Almighty will bless our union,
And through us, our families.
This vow represents my solemn commitment
To respect myself and you,
Our marriage and family,
And to pursue our continued growth
As a proud couple of African ancestry.

Part 4

Libations, Prayers, and Toasts

If you don't get married and have children, who will pour libations to you, who will remember you?

AFRICAN PROVERB

Libations

▼▼▼▼▼▼▼▼▼▼▼▼▼▼▼▼▼▼▼▼▼▼▼▼

The 1993 wedding service of the Rev. Patrick Keen and his bride, Katherine, opened

with a drum call. Dancers and drummers led the wedding party into the sanctuary, as Rev.

Emmanuel Grantson poured libations to the Creator and the ancestors to welcome their

spirits to the celebration. He called on them to bring peace and good wishes to the

ceremony, to rid the room of any bad spirits. And he asked the ancestors to use their spirit

to guide the ceremony and to alter the evil intentions of anyone who came wishing the

couple anything other than good.   Rev. Grantson was performing a custom that

dates back to antiquity. A libation quite simply is a prayer used in traditional African life.

Unlike western prayers, where the eyes are closed, libations are done with eyes open to

see what God has brought. Performed at significant events, such as a birth of a child, a

harvest, or a wedding, the pouring of libations as the first act in a wedding ceremony

honors the new life that the conjugal couple will bring into the world.   "The

ability to invoke spirits is innate in every human being," Rev. Grantson says. By lifting a cup to God and spilling a liquid on the ground, Africans use the material to bring together the Spirit to benefit human beings.

Linking the Circle of Life

According to Morris F. X. Jeff Jr., founder of Sankofa Communiversity, an African-centered university in New Orleans, the pouring of libations is a long-standing African tradition born of the knowledge that life never dies. "Everything that lives returns to its source. The source of life—our ancestral heritage—is revealed again and over again to the world. Thus life is a circle. In that circle, there is no distinction between past, present, and future."

In Africa, the libation serves several purposes. It calls on ancestral spirits, divinities, nature, and God or the Supreme Being to take part in the ceremony. It asks their blessing and guidance on behalf of the couple. It invokes ancestors to complete the circle that links a couple to the cycles of nature, to the unborn and the dead. The African philosophy requires that every celebration must invite the entire family to celebrate—to join hands with past, present, and future.

"It is the call of *umoja*, a call for the encircling of all of the living forms of life itself. The long life and the good life is the life of the living dead and spirit. The longer you are in spirit form, each day you're getting closer and closer to returning to your source—to the Creator," says Jeff.

There is a hierarchy to pouring libations that is strictly followed in African societies. The libation closely follows the family lineage, and in many cases, it is a recitation of a couple's links to each family member, living, dead, and unborn.

"The act of pouring libations is to reorder the circle of life and living," says Jeff, "to connect those ancestors who gave the first blood, and who lived and died to establish a foundation for us to live by and whose names we may not remember. Those ancestors are our spirit ancestors.

"Then there are ancestors who lived and died, and shared their eggs and seeds, blood, sweat, and tears with us, whose shoulders we stand on and whose names we do remember. Those are the ancestors who have made a contribution to the development of a family and to the African community, no matter where they are in the diaspora," Jeff continues.

"Then there are the elders who have received the gift of life from our living-dead ancestors whose names we remember. We give honor to those living elders—the great-grandparents, the grandparents, and the parents who carry the mantle of the seeds that were originally planted by the spirit forces whose names we do not remember, by those persons who have passed but whose names we do remember. Those elders who have passed their seed on to the living generation before us, the children and their children. Then there is the spirit that will emerge again in life, the children who are yet unborn. So you can see the full circle."

How to Create a Libation

A libation can be one of the most dramatic parts of a wedding celebration. It may be done at the ceremony and again at the reception. It is meaningful and colorful, and offers a moment to pause and reflect on the importance of family. It is an important act of remembrance that helps young people reclaim their family heritage.

Because it is prayer, it can evoke powerful emotions and feelings of good wishes. It also offers a way to highlight both families' ties to one another. The libation can be a way of elevating the event and involving guests and family members in a personal way. And for anyone who has lost a parent or other family, it can be a moment of emotional reconciliation and celebration.

Start by researching your family tree. Learn who your ancestors are and what contributions they made to your family. Because libations recognize those who lived with honor, be sure to acknowledge those who were teachers, activists, nurturers, or trailblazers. Note their place in the family circle and recite their relationship to everyone. Feel free to include those family friends who were close enough to be considered family.

Use African or African-American proverbs to spice up your libation. Or collect words of wisdom from family elders. Feel free to use words that have been passed down through the generations. Many of them still offer instruction for modern living.

Ask a grandparent or another family elder or trusted friend to give the libation. Use a gourd or calabash or wooden cup to pour. Fill it with water or wine. If done indoors, make sure there is a pot or bowl of earth in which to pour the libation, as it must be poured into the earth to reach the ancestors.

Feel free to include historical figures. Research figures from Africa and the United States or the Caribbean. Find out what their contribution to the community was. Acknowledge those ancestors who survived the middle passage. Call the names of the ancestors and explain why they were important; pour the liquid after each recitation. Include the libation you plan to use in the invitation or the wedding program so people can be familiar with the ritual at the wedding.

Make sure to recite the libation, then pour. After the libation is done, pass the cup among family members at the altar.

To start a libation, always start with God, next call on ancestors that the eldest person in the family would not remember—middle-passage voyagers, slaves. Include elements of Mother Nature in the libation, as it is considered part of the natural order of life. Next call those you want to remember. Your departed grandparents, aunts, and uncles are considered the living dead and a family's intermediary to God. Then call on the family elders. Mention your parents, uncles, aunts, family friends. Include here family members who were unable to attend the ceremony.

Also name the children attending and ask a special wish for the children to come in the marriage.

A libation, like a prayer, starts with an invocation to invite everyone to participate in it. It is followed by an introduction, where ancestors, elders, and family members are named. The supplication asks God for good wishes. The conclusion ends the libation by thanking everyone for participating. It also sends the spirits home.

Libation as Communion

Libation customs differ among the various African countries and villages. In South Africa, for instance, a libation may be accompanied by an offering. A cow will be slaughtered and its blood spilled on the earth. And people will place food and alcohol in a corner for the ancestors.

The Yoruba of Nigeria break kola nuts. Some they throw on the ground to the ancestors; the rest they share with people attending the affair.

In other families, food is prepared and a plate set aside for the ancestors. All the offerings are considered acts of communion and remembrance.

Libations come from the same cultural wellspring that gave us communion. As a sacred communal ritual, it helps to bind families and communities with everything that lives and everything that ever lived. It is also an act of remembrance to keep families linked to their familial legacy and to prevent them from becoming isolated and adrift in society.

Like the wine in communion, liquids are often used in libation. Some will include water, as a symbol of the continuity of life; some may use palm wine or palm oil, an essential household staple in Nigeria. Others may use coconut milk, a liquid that many consider a symbol of the mysteries in life. Other communities may use beer, gin, schnapps, or other alcoholic beverages as a symbol of the ancestral spirits. In Ghana, Rev. Grantson says, liquor is often used, as are rum, sorghum, millet, or corn. The liquid is poured symbolically on hallowed ground as an offering for the ancestors, and the rest shared by the wedding party and guests. Sharing the libation liquid reinforces the interdependence of the ancestors and the living family.

Libation Protocol

Libations can be simple expressions of good wishes or complicated choreopoems with refrains of call and response. In African society, every adult is expected to be able to call up the appropriate words at appropriate moments. It may be performed by the eldest family member or by a respected family member or friend. The officiant may be accompanied by instruments—bells, drums, horns. Repetition helps to reinforce sentiments and mood. A typical wish is "May the spirits on high, as well as the spirits below, fill you with grace."

Detroit-based Yoruba high priestess Queen Mother Dr. Osun Dara Nefertiti says she starts a libation by calling upon the Almighty Creator, God the father, God the mother, God of the universe, and orishas or ancestral spirits. Then she calls upon family members on both sides. The eldest person will call out the names of their ancestors or will ask family members to call on them, starting with family members on the woman's side.

"After they call upon family members, I let people from the audience call on people from the ancestors, from kings and queens of Africa, my family members, and those ancestors who those of us remember. When I nod my head, it means no one else is to call ancestors. Or I raise an *irukere* [horse tail]." She ends the libation by saying, "For all those ancestors whose names have not been spoken, may they continue to come in peace and help us. Ashe, amen, amenra."

The ending of a libation is as important as the invocation, says Morris Jeff. "If you invoke the ancestors to come—and they will come if you call them—after the celebration is over you must have a benediction to thank them for coming. And tell them that it is all right to go back and be ready to come back again when you call. If you don't give that recognition, they will stay. You must acknowl

DARYL PERRY
AND THERESA
PARRIS-PERRY
WEAR EMBROI-
DERED AFRICAN
CLOTH FOR
THEIR ATTIRE
IN A YORUBA-
INFLUENCED
CEREMONY.

edge and give them some instructions. Nothing is worse than an idle spirit."

Invocations

Following are several invocations that can be used while pouring libations at wedding ceremonies.

Kinship and Marriage Among the Anlo Ewe, by G. K. Nukunya, offered this libation, which is typical of ones used by families in Ghana and Togo.

> Today is an important day for us, the living, and it is fitting that we call you also, our ancestors, grandfathers, and grandmothers to come and join us on this occasion. The reason for our appeal is a good one. Your son has asked Imani to be his partner and this evening we shall have the consummation at the seclusion ceremonies. A successful marriage is realized in good health and fertility and prosperity. We therefore ask for our new couple a long life. Let them live till gray hair appears in their teeth and have as many children as possible. In commemoration of these requests, we offer you alcohol and cool water, for all of you to drink. You know everything. You can see the invisible. Perish our enemies and let our benefactors flourish. Once more here is water. We call all of you to come and drink.

The libation is poured and the rest shared among the family members.

This selection incorporates Yoruba customs.

> *Here is water to purify your home,*
> *Here's honey to sweeten your life,*

Here are kola nuts to test your strength.
Praise God,
Praise the spirits,
Praise the ancestors.
May God watch over you,
May your African ancestors give you guidance,
May your slave ancestors give you strength,
May your parents give you wisdom,
May your children bring you joy,
May you live in peace and harmony.

This descriptive and lyrical libation was created by Morris Jeff, who has incorporated African customs into his social work practice in New Orleans. It blends African and African-American historical figures as part of its ancestral call.

I pour *tambiko*—pure water—into the soil to awaken all spirits of the living dead who have provided foundation for us to survive and flourish in the world. We give homage to the Creator for being the source and aim of all life, all that lives and that ever lived. We thank the Creator for giving us life and giving us our ancestors.

We pour the libations for our ancestral spirits. Those who through their egg and seed united and brought forth our original life. Though we don't remember them by name, we remember their deed, for without their deed there is no fruition of our living on earth today.

We call upon the living-dead ancestors whose names we remember, and who we know not only gave us the opportunity for life, and who made the sacrifice to fight for us on the African shores—against our being severed and sliced and separated from our African homeland. We recall those brothers and sisters who took leadership roles in uniting us—Menes the first ruler of the first dynasty who merged upper and lower Egypt. We recall Hatshep-sut, the queen who united the crown—and as a female was king and queen sitting on the throne. And Shaka, the Zulu whose military might warded off European invaders.

Because marriage is a reuniting of those who have made an effort to reunify us, we recall and honor those who made a difference. In the United States, we call upon Harriet Tubman, the conductor who led slaves to the train of freedom. We call Sojourner Truth, an abolitionist and conductor on the Underground Railroad, whose words gave us hope and meaning. We call Fannie Lou Hamer, who fought for our right to vote when that right was not assured.

We call on Booker T. Washington, whose support for self-determination led him to found the Tuskegee Insti-tute to give African Americans the skills they needed to earn a living. W.E.B. Du Bois, who was born a slave and became a statesman and a founder of the NAACP, who encouraged us to take our place as intellectuals.

We recall all of our ancestors whose names we remem-ber and who we know through their history fought for our right to be in oneness with our God. Our right to be in oneness with the universe. Our right to stand erect as human beings with the rest of the human world. That lin-eage goes on as we recall Medgar Evers, a civil rights leader who braved death threats and taunts, only to be ambushed and assassinated one night as he returned home to his fam-ily. And the Rev. Dr. Martin Luther King Jr., who led the nonviolent charge that allowed us to dare to live our dreams. We recall Malcolm X, who was reborn in prison to lead us to honor our blackness and to understand the need to stand on our own as black men and women.

We call out the names of our family members who are among the living dead—those whose names we remember. We call upon those who started the foundation of these two families. We ask the families to call them by name. Next we call the names of our elders who are alive today and who are making a difference in our lives.

Now we call upon friends and folks related to the family. This call is to broaden the circle so we reunite, so we remember, so we recall. So we commune together in oneness.

Then we give homage to the mother and father of the couple getting married. For brothers and sisters who are not here, we ask that they be here in spirit. Then we pour libations for the children. Those who are amongst us, the young ones who are just born, and those who are yet to be born. We end our call with *harambee*—call for unity. Harambee is a symbolic act to draw our ancestors ever closer to us. We repeat harambee seven times because seven is considered a perfect unity. Hold the final harambee as long and loud as you can. It's an exhaling, a final act of unity. Harambee. Harambee. Harambee. Harambee. Harambee. Harambee. Harambee.

This African prayer signifies the importance of assembling the ancestral spirits at a daughter's wedding.

O Father, forebear of my daughter, this is the ox that we are sacrificing for you. Go up to the mountains, call your servants, assemble all your people for this banquet, all your warriors. This is your ox, chosen for your people. Sit and eat it, you and your people.*

The lively call-and-response feature of this libation is an invitation to the family and friends to become actively involved in the service.

---

*From *Prayers of African Religion* by John S. Mbiti (London: SPCK, 1975; New York: Orbis, 1976).

Officiant: Agoo.

Response: Ameh.

Officiant: Agoo.

Response: Ameh.

Officiant: Agoo.

Response: Ameh.

Officiant:

To God of our fathers, to God of our mothers.

To God Almighty who created the heaven and the earth.

To God who makes the sun rise and set.

To God who makes the thunder and lightning.

To God, the master of all things.

To God, who is everywhere.

We lift our voices to you.

This libation is in your honor,

And in honor of our ancestors who have lived and died
before us.

Grandfathers and grandmothers, we ask that you come
today.

To help us complete the circle of our family.

Our request is a humble one.

On this day of marriage

Two of your children have come to stand before the
family

To ask your blessing on their wedding day.

We petition for your wisdom to light our path, we petition for your protection to guard against evil, we
petition for your love to cherish in our hearts.

We pour this libation for the kings and queens of Africa,
from whom we descended.

We pour this libation for the ancestors, stolen, enslaved,
and freed, from whom we get our strength.

We pour this libation for our grandparents, from whom
we got our legacy.

We pour this libation for Grandmother Ella, from whom
    the Scott, Harris, Ford clan descended.
We pour this libation for Leora and Abbe Hammond,
    from whom the Hammond family descended. We
    pour this libation for Jimmie Sturgis, father of the
    Sturgis clan.
We pour this libation for Modestine and Edmund, par-
    ents of the Lake clan.
We pour this libation for our elders—Ozia Sturgis, Sarah
    and Frank Lake, who made a way for us.
We pour this libation for the children here and the chil-
    dren yet unborn.
We pour this libation for the couple being united today
    —Imani and Gyasi, who have heard God's call to
    unite and expand the family.
We pour this libation to complete the circle and to unite
    all our family members—the living, the dead, the
    unborn.
Ashe.
Response: Ashe.

This detailed libation helps to explain each facet of the ritual. It would be a good choice for a ceremony at which people are unfamiliar with African customs. It covers the purpose of libation and explains the various elements of it, as well as suggesting important historical figures whom it might be appropriate to mention.

An African proverb tells us that people who lack the knowledge of their past are like a tree without roots. It is in the spirit of remembrance that we pour this libation. We pour in honor of Sankofa, a word that means "Go back and fetch it," or learn from the past. There is a saying that he who is not taught by his mother is taught by the world. We pour this libation so that we may show our children the importance of family.

Ashe.

We use both hands to raise our cup to God to show our reverence for the original source of our lives. We use cool water to freshen the road our ancestors may use to travel to be here with us. We use cool water, also as a symbol of the continuity of life, to purify and to nourish our souls.

Ashe.

As a libation is an act of communion, of unity, we pour to celebrate the coming together of the families of Imani and Gyasi. It is said that through others, we are somebody. Through our actions, we broaden the circle to reunite our families, to remember our heritage, and to recall those who gave us life.

Ashe.

We call upon the living dead, our ancestors—our grandmothers and great-grandmothers, our grandfathers and our great-grandfathers—the forebears who are the foundation of our families. Immortalized in our thoughts, we call them by name: Leora, Jimmie, Ella, Modestine, Edmund. Though dead, they are alive in our memories. We call them the living dead.

Ashe.

We also call upon all those who gave their lives so that we may be free. We call upon François Dominique Toussaint L'Ouverture, the military genius who led slaves to persevere in their rebellion against Haiti, and journalist and anti-lynching advocate Ida B. Wells Barnett.

Ashe.

We call upon those who taught us to love ourselves and our culture. We call upon poets Langston Hughes and Paul Laurence Dunbar, folk historian and writer Zora

Neale Hurston, athlete, Shakespearean actor, and concert singer Paul Robeson.

Ashe.

We call upon our elders, whose wisdom we seek in all our endeavors. Those friends who have a privileged place in our family, and our parents, whose steady hand guided us along the bumpy road to adulthood. We call upon family members who would have been here if they could. We ask that they be with us here in our thoughts.

Ashe.

We call upon the bride and groom, may they always find prosperity in love and devotion. And we call upon the children, whose lives and well-being we are responsible for. Because children give glory to a home, we ask that this couple be blessed by children. We cast our libations to north, to south, to the east, and to the west.

Ashe, ashe, ashe.

This selection details the importance of immortality in libation rituals.

We call upon our own name seven times so one day we may be immortalized in the memory of our children as our ancestors are now. We invite God to look down upon his children as they gather for a day of honor, rejoicing, and remembrance. We ask for your blessing of power and unity. We honor our ancestors and ask those who have a foot in both worlds to carry our blessing to God so that he may hear our entreaties. We lift our voices to all whose bravery, blessings, perseverance, and deeds served to uplift and strengthen these families. We lift our voices to unite these two families. We lift our voices to banish ill will. We lift our voices to bring peace. We wish everyone to leave more blessed than when they came.

Prayers

*Entreat me not to leave you or return from
loving you. Where you go I will go. Where you live
I will live. Your people shall be my people.
And your God shall be my God.*

RUTH 1:16

While many wedding ceremonies may follow a standard and recognizable format, the

prayers contained within them allow the minister or officiant to personalize each service.

Used to bridge the various parts of a ceremony, the prayers serve to create and change

the service's moods and focal points. The right words can focus a spotlight on the bride

and groom. Then they can broaden the spiritual beam to encompass the family and the

community. Many of the ministers interviewed said that they are led by the spirit of God

to find the precise words to bring meaning and eloquence to every service.   For

ministers, wedding prayers offer a particular challenge and opportunity. They may be

charged with presiding over ceremonies for couples they know very well as well as for

others with whom they have only a passing acquaintance. By the nature of the ceremony, the prayers must relate to the personal and private relationship a couple has with God, yet be delivered in one of the most public of rituals. The prayers allow the minister to address God on behalf of the bride and groom, yet the couple is present to witness the minister's exhortations for them. The prayers must address private matters between the bride and groom, yet not hold them up for ridicule or speculation.

A ceremony may include several prayerful interludes. At the beginning of a wedding service, an invocation sets the meditative tone. As an invitation to the divine to take charge of the wedding service, it asks God to recognize and support the actions of the couple. It also asks the guests and family to give their blessing to the grand moment of consequence that the couple are undertaking.

The consecration exalts the wedding message. It creates a spiritual bond between the couple and God and offers a transition from the public spectacle to the intimate presentation of vows.

The final prayer of benediction evokes God's guidance and protection. The benediction offers a ceremonial climax to the service. It returns the intimate presentation to the community celebration. A minister's voice will rise with passion as he offers the prayers to uplift the new relationship that has been sanctioned by God and family.

Ministerial Prayers

Wedding prayers afford an unusual opportunity to address the Divine on behalf of the wedding party, and to address the wedding party, which has an opportunity to eavesdrop on the conversation between the one praying and God, says the Rev. Larry Williams of First Baptist Church of Lincoln Gardens in Somerset, New Jersey.

As former military chaplain, Rev. Williams has performed perhaps a larger number of weddings than the average minister, particularly on Valentine's Day, which soldiers have favored as a romantic date for matrimony.

"I've had as many as seven weddings a day on Valentine's Day," Rev. Williams said. His challenge on such a busy occasion was to make each ceremony unique and as personal as possible for each couple, even for those he knew very little about. He tried to make each prayer a singular and meaningful gift to each couple. "Wedding prayers are like a Dizzy Gillespie solo," said Rev. Williams. "I can't do it twice."

But within each prayer, Rev. Williams offers specific attention to personal attributes of the bride and groom to acknowledge God's gift to the couple.

"I would like to be able to address some specific issues in the prayer concerning the lives of the bride and groom," he said. "If I have any idea about a particular struggle they have known or some particular aspiration they have, or some hopes and dreams, I'd like to weave some notion of that into the prayer in the most subtle way possible. I would like them to be able to recognize it as they over-hear this prayer, but I would not like other people to recognize it, because it should be something that is private, especially when I think of myself as praying on their behalf.

"I want to express gratitude for the gift of marriage, for the gift of the relationship between husbands and wives. I want to acknowl-edge God as the giver of this gift of each to the other. And it's important to do that in my mind for the sake of having people acknowledge one another as worthy of treasure.

"One of the things we talk about in the preparation phase is the language we will use, and one of the key words we use in the cere-mony is cherish—love, cherish. It's easy for people to *think* about what they mean by love, but it's much harder to *say* it. Even more complicated than that is saying what they mean by cherish. So I like to have people come to a mutual appreciation for the meaning of that language, and then I want to weave into the prayers their val-ues as I have heard them expressed through the counseling, because I think it helps to make the ceremony a memorable experience."

For the Rev. Frank Smith, wedding prayers are an opportunity to bring to the ceremony what the Bible teaches about marriage.

"I'm trying to convey a Christ-centered attention. I'm asking Christ to sanctify this union and to convey to the participants and those watching that they are joined together by God. What I use is specific to the couple, what I've learned about the two people. I always take my focus beyond the event I've targeted, toward what my call is, to witness, to share Christ. Those things I say I don't only have to say to the couple but to plant in their perception the seeds of the value of Christ in their lives. Because I am a preacher, I am concerned about their souls' salvation."

But a prayer can be done by anyone. Performed by members of the wedding party, it can offer a personal blessing for the couple and the rest of the wedding party. Done by a parent or sister or brother, prayers become a familial link to an emotional and uplifting day. The prayers included in this chapter can be included in a wedding ceremony by a family member or a minister. Or they may be printed in the wedding program.

The prayers span the various parts of the ceremony. For example, "A Marriage Prayer" may be used as a benediction. The best man's prayer may be said before the ceremony starts. The prayers created by W.E.B. Du Bois are of a more general nature, but they may be adapted and used to incorporate a historical detail in a ceremony.

An Offering of Prayers

A Marriage Prayer by Lewis Garnett Jordan (1929)

Our Father, who art in heaven, who hast, in thy wise and tender care for mankind, ordained and blessed the institution of matrimony, we pray Thee graciously to regard Thy servant and handmaiden, who have thus solemnly pledged themselves to each other, and sworn unto Thee; that, through Thy good care and guidance, they may evermore remember and keep these their vows; be kept themselves in unbroken concord and sympathy all the days of their earthly lives; and be at last, with all most near and most dear unto them, gathered in an unbroken household to Thy right hand on the day of judgment. And may all of us, here assembled, be of that blessed company who shall be called to go into the Marriage Supper of the Lamb. And this we ask, only in the name and through the merits of Him, thine own Son, the Lord Jesus Christ. Amen.

Lord, Bless This Marriage— A Prayer of Renewal by Ella Black

Lord, Imani and Gyasi have called family and friends around, to share with them the love by which they're bound;

To recommit to each other before God above, rejoining their hearts, renewing their love.

Help them, dear Lord, as these words they repeat: "For better or for worse"; this pledge help them keep.

Bind them together, dear Lord, as one; give grace to their marriage through Jesus, Your Son.

As they travel together this road of life, help them not to stumble under a burden of strife.

Walk with them, Lord, through each passing day; cause them to seek Your will and Your way.

Meet their every need from this very hour; consecrate their lives with your Holy power.

Shower them with blessings that come only from above, as they pledge to each other unconditional love.

Amen.

Several Prayers for the Wedding Party
by Rev. Edward L. Hunt

A prayer to be said by the groom's best man before the wedding starts:

Dear Lord, we come before you today on behalf of Gyasi, asking your blessing and requesting that you, O Lord, would be with him and bless him not only this day, but all the days of his life. I pray, O Lord, that you help him to be a good spiritual leader of the home he is about to establish in your name. Bless Gyasi, we pray. Amen.

A prayer to be said by a bridesmaid before the wedding:

Lord, we call upon your name, saying thank you for this day of love. We request that there be peace through-out the world for a few moments, long enough for some-one to question why. Lord, let it be told that this day has been ordained by you, a day of peace and love—and Lord, we pray that you allow this day be named for Imani. Amen.

An invocation at the altar when the bride has passed and all are still standing:

Lord, we ask your blessing upon this service and these who have gathered in this church today to witness the joining of two devoted hearts. Amen.

A wedding prayer at the end of the service before the bride and groom kiss:

Dear Lord, we thank you for this service for Imani and Gyasi, who have come here today before you with family and friends to express their love through the exchange of the wedding vows. We pray that you, O Lord, would bless them as they turn and begin their lives together as one in your sight.

We pray that you would grant them love, joy, and peace in the home they will establish. We pray that you will assist them in their tender adjustment to living together. We pray that if it is your will, you grant them the joy of children in their home.

Lord, we pray that you teach them that loving you does not take away from their love for each other.

We pray that you would be with Imani and Gyasi in all that they do; and Lord, let it be in your name we pray.

Amen.

A Wedding Prayer
by Rev. Larry Williams

All wise and almighty God, as we stand together in this place, we bow in submission to your will. For you have left, for our record, instructions that men and women should leave their fathers and mothers to be joined as husband and wife.

We are grateful to you for this institution of marriage. In this relation we enjoy the privileges by which we must accomplish the divine injunction "Be fruitful and multiply; subdue the earth and replenish it."

Now we stand together with these your servants, Imani and Gyasi. Grant unto them, we pray, such grace as will sustain them through all manners of circumstances. In their sorrow, give them hope. In their poverty, cause them to prosper. In despair, redeem them, and in dying, give them new life.

It is written in your word that the fruit of the womb is a gift from God. When the time is right, grant unto these the privilege and pleasure of stewardship of even the fruit of their loins. And in the time of their child rearing, be with them for strength.

Now Lord, as they reach the end of this earthly sojourn, may these be found then as now, clinging to each other but more clinging to your grace, your mercy, your promise of everlasting life. And when one shall see the eyes of the other close in death, grant that thy spirit should fill the empty spaces in their hearts, and by that same grace they be risen together with Christ, in whose name we pray.

Amen.

A Prayer of Commitment
by Rev. DeForest B. Soaries

Eternal God, we commit to you now these two lives that you are joining together. We pray that you will guide these your children into this new segment of their life journey and that you will enable them to always remain loyal to the vows that they have shared today.

We pray that the love they share will be as unconditional as the love that you possess for all of your children. We ask that the home they are now establishing will be a place of peace and a haven of rest.

Provide them with the resources that they need to sustain their physical and spiritual needs and give them the capacity to share their love with others.

We pray that you will undergird them with your Holy Spirit and give them the power that they need to walk and never get weary, to run and never faint.

In Jesus' name we pray.

Amen.

CEREMONIAL NOTES

African Americans use prayer like a letter to God, says Rev. Larry Williams. "It opens with a salutation: How are things with you, Lord? The writer talks about all the things he wants to be thankful for. A petitioner may thank God for his or her relationship and go from being thankful to apologetic. And that is the place where sin is confessed. After the confession of sin and assurance of pardon, the petitioner talks about things he or she wants, a wish list. Then in closing, 'I got to go now, God, and sometime later, and I don't really know when that's going to be but, boy, it will be great when I live in that land where the wicked cease from troubling, and the weary will be at rest, and the streets are paved with gold.' And that's where our prayers end, in that heavenly place," says Rev. Williams. "So it really is like a letter to God, and then we sign it: This is your servant's prayer . . . and by the way, say hello to Jesus. In Jesus' name. Amen."

Two Prayers
by W.E.B. Du Bois

Lord of the springtime, Father of flower,
field and fruit, smile on in these earnest days
*   when*
the work is heavy and the toil wearisome; lift up
*   our*
hearts, O God, to the things worthwhile—sunshine
*   and*
night, the dripping rain, the song of birds, books
*   and*
music, and the voices of our friends. Lift up our
*   hearts*
to these this night, O Father, and grant us Thy
*   peace.*
Amen.

Dear Lord, make us mindful of the little
things that grow and blossom
in these days to make the
world beautiful for us.
Teach us to revere in this world not simply
the great and impressive but all the
minute and myriad-sided beauty of field and
*   flower and tree.*
And as we worship these, so in our lives let us
strive not for the masterful and the spectacular,
*   but for the*
good and true, not for the thunder but for the
*   still small*
voice of duty.
Amen.

Two Prayers of Invocation

O God of tender mercies, who in thy wise providence created the institution of marriage so man and woman would not have to live alone, look with kindness upon these your children, Imani and Gyasi, that they may be joined in that honorable state of marriage that you have ordained as the perfect gift for man and woman.

Surround them with our prayers and let them come to be strengthened by your love to endure the trials and tribulations of matrimony. May they always be filled with your love to enjoy the fruits of matrimony.

We know, dear Lord, that man and woman were created by you. And that you placed them together so they would not grow lonely. Dear Lord, let them know the delight and tenderness of a marriage in which love and comfort are given freely. Let them know the endurance of a marriage in which both partners have room to grow but also the grace to commit themselves to each other. We know, dear Lord, that you created marriage as a place to nurture children in surroundings of love and safety. It strengthens the family and is the rock upon which society is built. Let them know a fruitful marriage when the time comes. Fill their home with the blessings of children. And we ask, dear gracious God, that on this their wedding day they come to live out your purpose with the help and support of this community of family and friends.

Amen.

We stretch out our arms to you, O Lord, to give thanks for the love that has brought Gyasi and Imani together on this, their sweet day of matrimony. For the magic of their love, for the trust in their hearts, and for the leap of faith that made them choose each other, please heap blessings upon this couple. God who seeks the best in people and fulfills all our desires, consecrate their wedding day. Smile down upon them with the warmth of your radiance. We ask that you grant them understanding, temperance, trust, and kindness. May they cherish each other all the days of their lives. Amen.

A Prayer of Benediction

We clap our hands with joy, O Lord, as these your two servants stand on the threshold of a new life under one of your most cherished covenants. Strengthen them in times of trouble so that they may lean on each other. Fill them with happiness so that their joy may overflow and flood the valleys of sorrow. Give Gyasi and Imani the grace to find forgiveness when the hurts come fast and furious. Give them the insight to acknowledge and forgive their flaws. May they raise their children to be a source of light and inspiration in their communities. And may they live in everlasting joy.

A Prayer of Benediction
by Rev. Ruben Conner

Sanction this ceremony and matrimony that you will be with this man and this woman. Give them a happy, joyous, and fruitful relationship throughout the rest of their lives, and may their relations bring honor and glory to you. Amen.

Toasts

▼▼▼▼▼▼▼▼▼▼▼▼▼▼▼▼▼▼▼▼▼▼▼

To have peace at home
And pleasure abroad,
Love your wife
And serve the Lord.

Guy Benjamin remembered that as a child on the Virgin Island of St. John, his father was renowned for the speeches and toasts he gave at weddings. In the Caribbean of days gone by, a wedding was a great public holiday. Social contact was often limited in those small communities, and a wedding was an opportunity for everyone to gather for a great celebration. Entire villages would attend a wedding of one of its residents. Neighbors would send gifts of butter, eggs, sugar, coffee, and rum. The families spent weeks helping to prepare the fish and meats, sorrel, pound cakes, tarts, and other sweets for the feast.

People would often travel by boat from one island to the next to attend the wedding. Custom had it that everyone wanted to make a grand wedding speech. And nearly everyone who came brought a greeting or good wishes and stood to present it at the reception. Some men became known in their villages as toast-masters. Guy's father was one of those esteemed for his oratory.

For every toast given, he said, his father had a word of reply. Of the many toasts that his father gave, Benjamin remembers this one clearly:

> *Roses are red,*
> *Violets are blue,*
> *Birds love sunshine and so I love you.*
> *I wish you health,*
> *I wish you wealth,*
> *I wish you peace in store;*
> *I wish you heaven after death—*
> *What can I wish you more?*

Similarly, Dr. Lamuel Stanislaus is sought after for his speech-making and toasts. He learned his skill as a child on the tiny island of Petite Martinique in Grenada and honed it over the years, partic-ularly when he was ambassador of Grenada to the United Nations. He is regularly called upon for his toastmaster skills as chairman of the Caribbean American Community Comprehensive Center in Brooklyn, New York.

Although he has made many toasts since childhood, Stanislaus says the ovation he got as a child on Petite Martinique from a toast he gave that was memorized from a book still reverberates in his memory. "My favorite is one I did as a child that I got from a book, and upon which I built. Even now I say it, but I choose my occasion. By any measure, I still repeat that toast and it goes over in a big way."

> The custom of making speeches at wedding festivities is going out of fashion. But I am sure there are many here present who will pardon and expect a few words from one like myself who has known and greatly esteemed both the bride and bridegroom. The purpose in marriage is the begetting of children, so, bride and bridegroom, I wish you children. First a baby girl and when her hair begins to

curl, I wish you next your baby boy. Before I sit down, however, I am tempted to say a few words about that wedding ring, which has played so important a part in today's ceremony, and that ring is never found to flaw or else to sever. So, bride and bridegroom, may your love be as endless proof and pure as gold forever.*

Making a Toast

A wedding toast or speech is a wonderful opportunity to send best wishes to the bridal couple. Today, parents, siblings, friends, bride, and groom are often called upon to say a few words at the wedding banquet. These moments can be precious and meaningful—if you have the right words on the tip of your tongue. A toast, like a libation, dates from ancient times. It is offered to invoke wishes of prosperity, health, and success and generally accompanied by the raising of a glass of wine or other beverage. It may include irreverent jokes or heartfelt sentiments or words of wisdom from ancient folk sayings, such as the African proverb "Let matrimony be like a fowl's clothing, not parted until death."

Although most people dread speaking in public, a wedding is an occasion at which nearly everyone may be called upon for a few words at one time or another. It's best to be prepared.

There are several simple preparations to make the public speech effortless. Dr. Stanislaus says, "Govern yourself by five *B*s: *Be b*right, *be b*rief, and *be* gone." Or, as the saying goes, "An address should be like a woman's dress: long enough to cover the subject, but short enough to be inviting and enticing."

Seek out bright, witty, humorous stories to include. Don't be downbeat, negative, or offensive. Remember, you are speaking to a

---

*Adapted from Robert Herrick, "A Ring Presented to Julia." From *The Poems of Robert Herrick* (New York: Oxford University Press, 1965).

mixed group of guests. Avoid being pompous or overly apologetic. Use colorful expressions and everyday language for emphasis. Avoid clichés and use short, snappy sentences. Feel free to use repetition and rhymes because they help to reinforce your point.

Speak with sincerity and honesty and share your personal history about your relationship with the bride and groom. "You want to convey love and happiness and success in everyday life that covers not only the wedding but their entire lifetime," according to Mark Brown, the 1995 world champion of public speaking for Toastmasters International. Include anecdotes about how the couple met. Brown's toast at his sister's wedding offered these sentiments: "You had complained when you were younger how cold it was in New York. You fled to the warmth of Florida and that warmth has turned out to be David, your husband. The warmth of that love produced this wedding day. You are here at the beginning of a new part of life stemming from the love you share. Continue the love and happiness and warm feelings that you will share. And may you produce fine young children as wonderful, loving, and kind as you are."

Love is always a wonderful subject. Talk about love and marriage. But feel free to include some comments about children and family life. Include stories about your childhood with the bride or groom. Incorporate interesting stories about grandparents or other relatives.

Toasts may be created from just about any source. They are a great way to lend an afrocentric note to a ceremony. Weave into your toasts African proverbs, a favorite poem, African-American folktales, words of wisdom from famous African Americans or family members. Offer details about the couple's successes and triumphs. If they come from another country, contrast customs in their homeland with those in the United States.

Find out interesting family facts. Benilde Little and Clifford Virgin have parents who together have been married for more than eighty years. Their best man interviewed their parents for the keys to a long, loving marriage. One parent said the key to a successful marriage is never go to bed angry. Another said you met as individuals but you have to learn to become a couple. Another said jokingly that the key to their long-standing marriage was that she worked nights for thirty-two years. A father said never separate during hard times.

The best man's preparations gave wonderful insight and the personal words lent a emotional note to the event. Benilde said he summed up their advice with these words: "Clifford and Benilde, you are Americans of African descent. You are educated, aware, financially secure, and intelligent. You have a legacy of a stable family. You have every reason to succeed. Today you are surrounded by approximately two hundred of your best friends and family members, people who love you perhaps as much as you love each other. I'd like for them to join me not in a wish but a demand that you make your marriage a success."

A Sampling of Toasts

FOR LOVE

Your love should be like that of Abraham and Sarah. Your love should be like that of Venus and Adonis. Bride and bridegroom, I am bringing to your attention these wonderful models upon which your love and your life should dwell.

Happy the bride and bridegroom and thrice happy are they whose love grows stronger day by day and whose union remains undissolved until the last day.

Blest and thrice blest are they whose love remains unbroken and whose existence will go from time to time and to end and for end everlasting.

HUMOROUS

Up to the nostrils, over, under, and around the tongue, tell the stomach look out, I am coming down. Good health to the bride and bridegroom.

Bride and bridegroom, I trust that the hinges of your love will never rust, and that the portals of your heart will remain safe and secure.

When you are married, you must obey,
You must obey in all you say;
So love each other like sister and brother,
And pay attention to kiss each other.

TRADITIONAL

A successful marriage is a journey and not a destination. That's why you have to keep working on it. Let us drink to your health and happiness.

Dark and stormy may come de wedder,
I jines dis he-male and she-male togedder;
Let none but Him dat makes de thunder,
Put dis he-male and she-male asunder;
I darfore 'nounce you bofe de same,
Be good, go 'long, and keep up you name.
De broomstick's jumped, de worl's not wide;
She's now you own, salute de bride.

TO SUCCESS

Bride and bridegroom, may you live as long as you want and want nothing as long as you live.

If you have much, give from your wealth; if you have little, give from your heart.

Here, take dis lil gift
And place it near your heart
It keep away dat lil riff
What causes folks to part.
It only jes a rabbit toe
But plenty luck it brings;

It worth a million dimes or more,
More 'n all de wedding rings.

KEYS TO A HAPPY MARRIAGE

Imani and Gyasi, congratulations on your wedding day. I know you are happy today, and may happiness follow you. To help you on the journey, I have taken the liberty of interviewing the experts—those married more than twenty years—about the keys to a happy marriage. There were many suggestions, but most of them boil down to just a few simple steps. According to this scientific survey, a happy marriage can be achieved if you:

1. Make a cheery disposition a lifelong habit.

2. Don't just keep happiness to yourself; spread it around.

3. Offer kindness but be able to accept it as well.

4. Be generous with your love but stingy with your criticisms.

5. Learn to trust and be trustworthy.

6. Treat your mate as you would your best friend.

7. Be willing to talk openly and honestly, but more important, be willing to listen.

8. Always stoke the embers of passion before they fade.

9. Keep a hearty hug handy.

10. Always fight fair but always be willing to lose.

Remember that African proverb: Receiving honor won't make you a ruler, and giving honor won't make you a slave.

FROM AFAR

May your love be like the misty rain, gentle coming in but flooding the river.

—Africa

If you want to live long with your wife, you must be patient.

—Yoruba

A good or bad husband makes little difference, but if the wife is good, then all is good.

—Kunama

TO HERITAGE

By jumping the broom, Imani and Gyasi have decided to take a leap of faith. That faith is the same as that our grandparents and great-grandparents had when they packed up and left the South on the slim belief that there were better times ahead. Their lives hold instruction for you newlyweds. Our folks didn't know where they were headed or where they would end up. Many trips are like that. All they knew was the time had come to make a change.

That leap of faith is what marriage is about. Like that journey, there will be rough times and hard times. Be like those northern-bound travelers—learn to lean on one another in times of trouble.

There will also be sweet times and fun times. Be like your elders and learn to laugh full out loud and deep and kick up your heels when the music is good.

Those old folks didn't have a lot of money, but they didn't waste what they had. Be like those old folks—learn to be resourceful and when money is tight, pool your resources.

Those old people knew that children were important for the future. They made sure we got a good education in schools that didn't want us. They made sure we got to church when we didn't want to go. And they made sure that no child went unsupervised if their parents had to work. Be like those elders and treat your children like the blessings that they are.

Despite their struggles and sometimes despair, those northern-bound travelers look back on their lives as a great adventure and talk about the good old days. My wish for you is the same as those old folks experienced: May the afterglow of memory always reflect warmly on your life together.

Part 5

Reaffirming Marriage

*So men ought to love their wives
as their own bodies. He that
loveth his wife loveth himself.*

EPHESIANS 6:28

Couples Speak of Love and Devotion

▼ ▼

The Legacy of Marriage

In another era, marriage was essential for the collective survival of a clan. Men and women bonded together to increase their family's protection against a common enemy, be it human, animal, or nature. Our ancestors learned then that couples who made the most of their interdependence could increase their social and economic standing through an extended family system. Marriage was the stabilizing force that helped a clan survive and thrive against all odds. Through the ages, families and the larger community have been strengthened by men and women who worked toward a shared purpose.

It was this tradition that helped millions of Africans survive the brutality of the middle passage, slavery, and emancipation. As slave traders sold and transported Africans throughout the Caribbean, the United States, and South America, those ingrained customs helped families endure the harsh life of slavery and estrangement.

For African Americans, slavery was a troubling time for marriages and families. Though prevented from marrying by their slave masters, and separated by the auction sale or a dangerous flight to freedom, men and women still chose partners and many remained faithful.

Sociologists have documented the breakdown of marriage and black family ties during slavery as husband, wife, and children were separated and sold in separate lots. Many attribute our marital troubles today to that peculiar institution. However, many of those marriages proved resilient despite inhospitable surroundings and hostile treatment. That the marriages of many African Americans were able to endure was a testimony to their ability to put aside personal desires for a common goal.

Against the Odds

Letters and notes gathered from slave narratives and government records offer a striking testimony to the power of love and faith. The missives include poignant letters written by slaves or dictated to scribes, in which men acknowledged their abiding commitment to their spouses.

Among many hundreds of letters that stand as a record of their commitment is that of escaped slave Samuel Washington Johnson, who was unwilling to relinquish his relationship even though his wife remained in bondage:

> I hope you will remember me now just as same as you did when I was there with you because my mind is with you night and day. The love that I bear for you in my breast is greater than I thought it was. If I had thought I had so much love for you I don't think I ever left, being

I have escape and fled into a land of freedom. I can but stop and look over my past life and say what a fool I was for staying in bondage as long. My dear wife, I don't want you to get married before you send me some letters, because I never shall get married until I see you again. My mind don't deceive and it appears to me as if I shall see you again.*

In another instance, Abream Scriven defied futility and was compelled to honor his family ties despite being sold away from them:

My dear wife I take the pleasure of writing yo these few lines with much regret to inform you that I am sold to a man by the name of Peterson a treader and stays in new orleans. I am here yet but I expect to go before long but when I get there I will write and let you know where I am. My Dear I want to send you some things but I do not know who to send them by but I will try to get them to you and my children. Give my love to my father & mother and tell them good bye for me, and if we shall not meet in this world I hope to meet in heaven. My dear wife for you and for my children my pen cannot express the griffe I feel to be parted from you all.

I remain your truly husband until death.†

After emancipation, many slaves abandoned their plantations and traveled in droves to search for lost spouses and family members. Many became surrogate fathers and mothers and extended families for the children they found along the way. Other men and women, who had jumped the broom, sought to further legitimize

*From *The Black Family in Slavery and Freedom: 1750–1925*, by Herbert G. Gutman (New York: Pantheon Books, 1976).

†From *Blacks in Bondage: Letters of American Slaves*, Robert S. Starobin, ed. (Princeton, N.J.: Wiener, Markus Publishers, Inc., 1988).

their union by registering at the Freedman's Bureau when it became legal to do so. Elburt and Marien Williams of North Carolina, who were not able to travel, sent their marriage affidavit by envoy to have it registered at the Freedman's Bureau.

> I Elburt Williams and Marien Williams has been livin together 18 years & we do both affirm that we do want each other to live as man & wife the balance of life & being disable to walk & Marien being in the family way I will send this to you & you will please make it all wright with us.*

Still others who had married during slavery were able to celebrate the longevity of their union and the fall of servitude. In celebration of the golden wedding anniversary of Thomas and Annette Lathrop, a canticle was written for the 19th-century couple. They were married in the antebellum period on November 25, 1830, and celebrated their anniversary in 1880. Their marriage was unique not only in that it survived slavery, but also that it endured despite the hardships that African Americans faced during emancipation and Reconstruction.

Their minister said: "You have lived to see African slavery become a thing of the past, ground to impalpable dust by the onward march of God's chariot wheels, which never roll backward. You have lived to read by your own fireside the Emancipation Proclamation, which struck from the hand of the master the scourge, and from the captive forever the handcuff and the chain; which lifted four million of your race into the enjoyment of that richest and most priceless of all temporal blessings, personal freedom."†

---

*From *The Black Family in Slavery and Freedom*, by Herbert G. Gutman.

†From "Anniversary Record of the Golden Wedding of Mr. and Mrs. Thomas Lathrop" (Plainfield, Conn.: C. F. Burgess, printer, Journal Office, 1881). From the collection of Brown University Library.

Slavery's Lasting Legacy

But the impact of slavery cannot be discounted. Many families were dismantled and destroyed at their master's whim. Many never knew what it was to have a normal family relationship. Men and women, torn from their mates, found companionship with others, complicating family patterns and relationships.

Despite that, the number of marriages in the pre–civil rights era was strong as African-American men and women built communities. Everyone worked for a common good as extended family members joined resources to seek prosperity. During the 1960s and '70s, many black nationalists sought to create a new model for uniting African Americans and strengthening the black community. Haki and Safisha Madhubuti were married during that period and were among the cadre of people working to make changes in that era of cultural revolution.

Safisha states: "It is through marriage and families that communities are built and sustained and new generations are socialized. So it extends beyond the borders of individuals and individual feelings. We wanted a family. We wanted to raise children. We wanted to socialize a new generation. We wanted to create a model that we think was desperately needed.

"There's an awfully prevalent notion in contemporary American culture that marriage is about your heart beating and that it's purely individual. Just you and this person and your feelings about this person. And when any of those conditions of your individual feelings of the moment are not sustained, that you don't need to be in it anymore because it's individual. I don't believe people should stay in marriages when they're unhappy; I don't believe people should stay in marriages that are abusive, but you can't talk to anybody who's been married for a long time who won't tell you that they've had very difficult times. That they've had times when they were very unhappy. People stay together through those times because of an essential love, respect, and friendship that becomes the bedrock of the relationship. And because they share goals larger than them and the moment."

Today, however, in a period of phenomenal economic growth among the black middle class and more opportunities for African Americans than ever before, marriages are faltering. We hear daily stories of failed relationships, children set adrift by divorce, single mothers, homeless men.

Keeping the Commitment

With so many modern marriages falling by the wayside, it is important to acknowledge the ones that endure and thrive through better or worse. In the pages that follow are personal testimonies that speak of the triumph of marriage. Couples married for many years reflect on their lives together. They offer insight as to how they found their soul mates. And they testify to the fulfillment of their relationship despite the years, children, and public opinion.

There is a story by Chester Himes about the ends to which a couple goes to renew their feelings for each other. Himes is noted for his detective novel *Cotton Comes to Harlem,* which was turned into a movie in the 1960s. He also wrote short stories about relationships, including "A Modern Marriage," written in 1933.

There are also letters, poems, and readings about the uplifting and inspirational aspects of matrimony.

Couples today with successful marriages understand that love's resilience is born as much in struggle as in happiness. The people interviewed here come from a variety of economic backgrounds and professions, from blue collar to intellectual and from homemaker to professor. Their marriages, however, tell similar stories of finding common ground to build a strong relationship. These people are optimists. Instead of worrying about how many ways their partnership could dissolve, they have invested in making it stronger. Instead of pursuing independence, they welcomed an interdependence that allowed for and celebrated personal growth and common goals. They saw themselves as a team and nurtured the love that brought them together.

How They Knew

Barbara and Hank Jackson of Philadelphia, for example, have known each other nearly all their lives. Married in 1969, they grew up in the same neighborhood and attended the same Bible school and elementary school. Hank, a building contractor and construction carpenter, and Barbara, a member of the administrative team at Lotus Academy, were both born and raised in South Philadelphia about one and a half blocks from each other.

Hank became friends with Barbara's cousin, but it was a year before he really noticed her. Hank was sixteen, Barbara, thirteen.

"As we got older, she'd end up tagging along at parties," Hank said. "I went in the service and I was away for two years. I came back and hooked up with my best friend again, and his new wife. And Barbara went out with us. She was twenty-one and I was twenty-four and I saw her in a new light.

"We were friends. We were both physically attracted to each other. She still has a great smile. The real thing that brought us together was that we liked being around each other all the time. Even with the romantic involvements we had with others, we still always liked to be around each other because we had a good time together. If we were ever somewhere where she wanted to dance and nobody was asking her, she always knew she could ask me to dance. I kept turning around in this circle of friends and after a while the only people left in a circle were me and Barbara."

Barbara says: "One of the things that definitely attracted me to him was that he has a positive-type personality. He also has a great smile. His smiles still send butterflies through my stomach. At some point I knew it, that he was the one."

A Cause for Love

Poet, essayist, and publisher Haki Madhubuti and his wife, Safisha, met in a professional setting. Married twenty-two years, the Chicago couple met when they worked during the black nationalist movement. Haki was one of the founders of the African-centered cultural movement in the country, and Safisha, now a college professor, worked with him to build the Institute of Positive Education. The organization helped create a more afrocentric philosophy to guide black social institutions from marriage to education.

"We met when I was teaching at a local area high school and he had come to speak there," Safisha said. "We started talking. It was not long after that he brought a group of us together and talked about starting the Institute of Positive Education in 1969. We began working together to develop this organization and we became close.

"Haki is an exceptionally bright person, and one of the things that has always characterized our relationship is that I always felt as if I learned from him. He's a very kind person. He's thoughtful and sensitive. He thinks deeply. Those were qualities that drew me to him. Those were the qualities that sustained our relationship. Initially we were both young. He was handsome. He was a poet. It was easy to be attracted to him.

"I worked with him for five years intimately. I knew him very well, worked with him every day. I wrote him a letter and told him that I thought we had played around long enough and that I wanted to be married and that was a principal part of maintaining, continuing our relationship. If he wasn't ready, we could go our separate ways. I would continue working for the institute because it was work that I believed in. But we didn't have to keep seeing one another. I thought five years long enough."

Haki said he accepted her proposal without hesitation.

"I'm not a fool. If you look at a pool of women and you have a list of what you would like to have in a wife and someone to be with for a long time, she met all the criteria. We had been together for so long and we really just took the next step.

"As we worked together it became very clear that not only was she a woman I could communicate with at an intellectual and theoretical level, but also she was practical in how she saw the world and her position in the world.

"I was moved by the sensitivity that she has for children. She is a strong person, strong willed, and once she sets her mind to doing something, she does it without hesitation and she has a track record of accomplishments. Safisha came along at the right time."

Young Love That Lasts

Gwendolyn Mike of Orlando, Florida, fell for Roger when she was fifteen. Roger, a young, handsome musician, worked with a church boys' chorus.

She was in love with him for two years before he even knew who she was. "A friend asked me if I wanted to talk to Roger. We talked that day and the night before I left, we knew we wanted to get married. That's how it started. I knew I was in love with him already. I just needed him to tell me what he liked in a young lady. We like everything, do the same things, and eat the same things."

"Being popular and young at that time," Roger said, "I would travel from city to city in Florida and out of state with the boys' chorus. A friend introduced me to my wife. I went to another program and there she was. I decided I would sit and talk. I began to talk and discovered she could sing; she was a profound cook and had won a prize at a state fair for her cooking. She had her head together and was extremely neat and clean. She was unique and outstanding in her personality, and she was winning."

In their conversations, they discussed food and dress and children. They talked about Roger's choir duties. "There was one understanding that I was in the Lord and she had to be able to withstand a Christian setting," he said. "And could she withstand the importance of my music to me.

"I knew this was the woman after my third encounter with her," Roger said. "I went home and told my dad I had met the young lady I would marry one day. I said I am going to marry her because I love her."

They dated for six years. Because they lived in separate towns, they communicated by phone and by letter. They would meet at church affairs two or three times a year. She went to college in a town near him. But they broke up for one year when Roger left for California.

"I prayed about it for a long time," Roger said. "I went out to California to get away and test and see how it would turn out. I stayed true to her. I knew it was a terrible setback for her and she was determined to hold back with prayer."

They ultimately married on August 15, 1971, and recently celebrated their twenty-fifth wedding anniversary.

What Makes a Good Marriage?

The couples who make a success of their relationship accept their differences and share their strengths. They cater to each other to make sure that they can keep the love fires stoked day in and day out. When they they start to drift, the couples find ways to reconnect. But for most of them, their relationship starts with the personal values they share. They say having the same set of basic values gives them a solid basis for building a strong, long-lasting marriage.

Hank Jackson recalled talking to his father about those issues. "When I was fifteen, my father asked, 'Do you think I still love your mother? I don't really.'

"He said that my mother was the person he most admired and respected in the world and that she was his best friend. And whenever I get married, it should be on that basis. That someone's idea of romantic love doesn't really last past the blush of youth.

"I thought it was cold when he said it at that time. But that's basically the way Barbara and I got together. We were friends before we got married. And we are friends. If there's one single thing to point to, that would be it, our friendship.

"We could almost tell about our friends who got married which ones would last and which ones wouldn't, based on whether they were friends and whether or not they saw the same thing or had developed the same perspective," says Hank. "We did a lot of reading, discussing, seminars, and chose a direction reflected in the Nguzo Saba. We embarked on certain destinations together. I guess you can be friends if you are not of like minds. You have to be friends but almost have to be of like minds to make this kind of intimacy in marriage work."

Barbara agrees. "It's friendship, respect, and admiration. It won't work if you are not friends and don't respect each other. All the other things are nice and they are a part of it. But it's not the glue that holds it together. You're not always going to be lovey-dovey; you will have to get down and argue and you're going to disagree about certain things. You may do some things you don't want to do. He has to give in there. And I have to give in somewhere else. I know that when the dust clears, he's still going to be there for me. He still has my back just like I still have his, regardless of whatever happens. It's comfortable and comforting knowing that no matter what happens, he's going to be there for me."

The Jacksons say they have supported each other through years of growing pains and transitions. Hank particularly recalls with some chagrin his macho period early in their marriage. "I got into a macho role. I thought that was what a man was supposed to do. I do more of those kinds of things than I would have then, as far as fixing dinner and washing clothes. In our house, work didn't have a gender. As the children got older, we wanted to encourage them to do that. It's not only a role that we wanted the boys to see a woman in. It became clear that if I didn't do certain things, there would be no reason for my sons to learn them. The proper way of sharing is based on what has to be done.

"The strength in our relationship is that she hasn't held it against me that I was doing my macho posturing back in 1971 and '72. The role of black women has changed. And the role of black men has changed. We decided that whatever happens, it's together. We can't possibly do this with one of us going one way and one of us going the other. No matter what happens, we stick together."

The Art of Sharing

The theme of shared purpose resonates in the Madhubuti household as well. As a couple very much involved in the black movement, they have internalized their goals for the black family, and live according to their ideals. But they acknowledge having to work through difficult periods and anger the same as any couple. They work hard to combine their independent goals and shared responsibilities. For these two, their public work and their private lives are the substance of a cooperative and loving relationship.

"The core of values and those things that pushed us toward each other remain," says Haki Madhubuti. "The whole process of maturation means that things do change. Bodies change, energy levels change, bringing children to any relationship changes it. We have three children, two in college and one in high school. We live in a three-generation home and that has been positive. It's in keeping with the values we think are necessary. It's a good lesson for our children. They must understand that the family is of critical importance and that nothing comes before family.

"One thing that has always characterized our relationship is that we're two very productive people. I've always felt that few things will stop me from producing, building something that will ultimately benefit our national and local community. That's one of the reasons I worked so hard to make Third World Press a force.

"I found in Safisha a woman who has her own identity and her own ideas. It was critical to me. That's one of the reasons we've been able to stay together so long, because she has been able to develop her own space. We have our own space and even do our own work, at the same time sharing those things that are absolutely necessary, especially in the nurturing and raising of our children. And even sometimes intellectually in terms of our own work. We just published a small book together called *African-Centered Education*."

"You have to have deeply shared values," says Safisha. "I don't think you can have deep respect for somebody you don't share fundamental values with. You must always be respectful even when you may be hurting each other. There are some things that become lines that you don't cross. Because if you cross these lines, you can't come back. You have mutual understanding about what those things are. You try to do things to stroke each other, strengthen each other, and to support each other."

Gwen and Roger Mike say they try every day to make their lives as special as the day they married. "You make every day as exciting as you can as though it was your wedding day," says Roger. "We go to the grocery store together and I surprise her with a single rose. It's from the heart. I have hidden cards for her to find. My wife goes the extra mile to do the little things and I try to match it. I try to keep up with the dates and all activities of the calendar—Mother's Day, her birthday, Valentine's Day. We are there for each other."

Crafting Compromise

Compromise has been the hallmark of the forty-five-year relationship between Floyd and Etta McAfee. Despite the separations that occurred during Floyd's thirty-year career in the army, they both have been willing to adapt to change. "We had a lot of separations. He was gone so much, we were glad to see each other. It was always a honeymoon." The last ten years together since he has retired from

the military has been the most time they have been together con-
tinuously, says Etta. "I required a few adjustments. I didn't cook
that much. I had to get into a routine. I had to learn to say, 'Honey,
I'm going to the shopping mall.'"

Learning the art of compromise took time and much adjustment, says Etta. But it has resulted in a deeply enriching
relationship.

Compromise, she says, was a progressive thing. "You don't
know a person until you live with them. You have to able to see their
point of view and not be critical. The art of compromise is not about
demeaning or belittling yourself. It helps to get in sync with your
partner. If you truly love each other, you have a strong foundation
of mutual respect. He had to make a lot of adjustments. My husband
is an only child. He's very disciplined. I'm not. I'm an extrovert. He
had to get used to my ways and I had to get used to his.

"We truly enjoy each other and even today, he calls me as soon
as he gets to work. He says, 'Give me my hug to drive.' We are more
in love today than when we were married."

The McAfees are so in sync with each other's feelings that they
are able to sense each other's distress even over a distance. "When
something's not right I can feel it," she says. "He was in Iran and I
was at home with an impacted tooth removed. I was in so much
pain. He said, 'Honey, were you calling me last night? It seems like
you were stressed.' In that much distance he felt my pain.

"He was a man ahead of his time," Etta says. "He'd get up at
night with his children. He would change diapers, feed them. On
Saturdays, he'd tell me to get out of the house. That was his day to
spend with the children. It was my day off. I'd take one with me.
He'd bundle our daughter Flo up and the guys would say here
comes Mac and his baby. He was very involved with his children."

Love Guided by God

Making a place for spirituality in their lives is another important aspect for these successful couples. Although the Jacksons, for example, follow no prescribed religious tenets, like all the couples they abide by a solid spiritual core. Religion is the way you live, Hank says. "It's the way you relate to family, the way you relate to your mate, the way you relate to your friends, the environment. It means more to treat people correctly whether you go to church or not."

Ella and Robert Black met in college about 1959. Although they dated a bit, Robert eventually became engaged to someone else. After college they returned home and corresponded for several years. Robert's engagement eventually broke up and he renewed his relationship with Ella.

Today they team up as deacon and deaconess at Tenth Street Baptist Church in Washington, D.C., to work on a marriage ministry to strengthen relationships among the couples at church. Married thirty-three years, they call each other Sweetie.

"When the initial relationship broke off, it was not as if I was intent on getting married," said Ella, fifty-four. "I went on with life. When the relationship with the person he was engaged to fell apart, I was there when he came back. He came to visit. The thing about him that drew me was he respected me. He was a respectful person. He was kind, considerate. He was a gentleman. My parents liked him a lot."

Robert, fifty-six, said emerging doubts told him that his previous engagement was not going to work. "My imaginary person was not the one I was engaged to. The thing I had in mind was a person who was understanding, easygoing, a person who was cute, with a nice shape, interesting. Sweetie was an easy person to like because she was very lovable. She had a way that would draw a person to her. I enjoyed being around her. She proved to be the imaginary person. And I knew that."

The Blacks base their marriage and their ministry on the teachings of the Bible. They share strict biblical interpretation of marriage. "Many people believe there is a 50-50 role for a man and woman, and that is far from the truth. Marriage is a 100-100 relationship," says Robert Black.

"The marriage vows are a clear example. When the vows are given, the minister addresses the man first. He asks all the questions pertaining to the marriage vows. Before he turns to the woman, the man has to respond. He promises to love and take care of his mate. Technically speaking, he's married. From that moment he has agreed to do all these things although she has not agreed to all those things.

"Thereafter the minister turns to the woman to ask similar questions. The woman's answers are contingent upon the man's response of what he will do. Each person agrees that they will do what they say they will do. It's not based on whether she works. He is required to work whether she goes to work or not."

Robert Black says many couples get caught on the submissive role of the wife. He says in a Christian marriage, they both must be submissive to each other.

"First and foremost you should be a Christian. It is necessary to understand scriptural principles first. As believers in Christ, we have to be submissive to one another. Submissive goes a step further for the woman. Christ is head of husband, husband is head of wife. Most people might say my wife comes first. Christ should come first. If Christ doesn't come first there will be more flaws in the relationship."

Lasting Through Trying Times

The Rev. Edna Vaughn and her husband, Earnest, understand the true meaning of "Love conquers all." Married fifty years, the New Jersey couple have endured their share of heartache and illness. They have put their faith in God and trusted each other through many illnesses and setbacks. Both suffer from asbestosis and Edna has been ill during most of their marriage.

"I've been in hospital forty-four times, had sixteen operations, and suffered through a variety of ailments and operations, including a tonsillectomy, hysterectomy, foot operation, narcolepsy, stillborn twins. He would have to put his hands under my back and dress me. Through everything I had, Earnest stood by me. When I was hospitalized, he had to take three buses to see me. He never missed coming. He'd fall asleep at my bedside. Sometimes I would be in bed for three and four months at a time. He would make my breakfast, bring it to me, come home, cook, take care of the children. I don't take it lightly.

"He's a man who cannot stop working. When my church needs something, they call for him. He's making extra money all the time. Having raised such a large family, we don't have a lot of money, so it helps that he works all the time."

Edna says they've survived each crisis by cherishing each other. "God blessed us with a love that has kept us. Some things are ordained. He has stuck by my side. Even after fifty years we think it's not robbery to hold hands, to touch, to kiss. He makes me feel like Cleopatra. We don't see a life without each other. We are filled with asbestos. God has blessed me with a strength that I can't explain. My husband didn't have any schooling. He only went to the eighth grade. He's an old-fashioned man; he handed me his pay envelope from the first week we got married. He has trusted me for fifty years to handle the money.

"I've always taken care of everything. My husband didn't write a check. He used to never dial a phone. Now everything is in his hands because I am not well. Now he's taking care of everything.

"When I looked my worst, he'd hold me and tell me how much he loved me. I'm old and broken down and he never tires of me."

Words of Renewal

Perhaps because people are so aware of how often marriages fail, more and more of them are seeking to reaffirm and renew their promises to each other in formal ceremonies. People from all walks of life are taking time to stop to reflect on their lives together. Even actor Denzel Washington and his wife, Pauletta, renewed their vows in a South African ceremony presided over by Bishop Desmond Tutu. Ministers across the country are finding an increase in the number of renewal ceremonies they perform. And more people are seeking marital workshops to better understand each other and to learn to iron out problems before they become overwhelming. Churches are holding weekend retreats and workshops for singles and married couples. There is a newfound effort to find grounds of support rather than grounds for divorce. Marriage renewal ceremonies have become a popular feature at the Black Family Reunions that have been held throughout the country. The Jacksons renewed their wedding vows with seven other couples at such an affair in Philadelphia in 1993. "A friend of ours had recommended it. I thought it was a good idea," says Hank. "There wasn't a lot of beforehand preparation. We are thinking about doing it again for our thirtieth anniversary two years from now."

The Mikes had a renewal ceremony in August 1996 that was several times larger than the modest nuptials they had twenty-five years ago. This time their celebration featured an African-centered ceremony. As a tribute to his wife, Roger composed an album of love and wedding music. The ceremony included a hundred-voice chorus with musicians who came from Georgia and Alabama to play.

With the help of their friend Olga Byll, originally from Togo, Gwen was responsible for the food and the attire. Her ensemble was a white *boubou* trimmed in gold. "I wanted it to be a unique wedding, something that everybody who attended would remember,"

GWEN AND
ROGER MIKE
AND THEIR
TWENTY-FIFTH
ANNIVERSARY
WEDDING
PARTY

said Gwen. And no doubt it was, with a planned wedding party of thirty-six, including twenty-five of the children they raised, from four to twenty-six, in the wedding party as bridesmaids, ushers, flower girls, and Bible bearer.

Robert and Ella Black have seen an increase in the number of people who participate in the workshops they lead. "When we started in '92," said Ella, "the first thing we did was a sweetheart banquet. We ate, we played games, had entertainment. We had a testimony from a couple who had been separated for ten years and who renewed their vows. We got an idea for an annual enrichment ceremony; our pastor did the first ones. We talked about communication, sexual relationships, child rearing, the relationship of the two parties with God, the roles of the man and woman. It was four nights of role playing, lots of couple interaction. People really enjoyed and appreciated it. I guess the telling thing is that they come back every year and it has grown. And marriages have been helped."

For the Blacks, the reward for helping others in their church's marriage ministry has allowed them to better understand their lives together. They renew their vows at nearly every renewal program that they lead.

"God has given every Christian a gift. One of our gifts is helping other people in marriage. As we shared what we were doing, people would come to us to ask for advice. From there was the start and we just became the unofficial marriage counselors at church," said Robert.

"The reasons for the seminar are to reaffirm and to teach other things about the marriage relationship. We hope couples will come away and be reminded and be committed to put in practice the things they have learned. They learn to be more responsive to each other's needs. We ask who wants to make the recommitment. When people agree, it's because they've come to a new place to be responsive in their relationship."

The Union of Two
by Haki Madhubuti
For Ife and Jake

What matters is the renewing and long-running
   kinship
seeking common mission, willing work, memory,
   melody, song.

marriage is an art,
created by the serious, enjoyed by the mature,
watered with morning and evening promises.

those who grow into love
remain anchored
like egyptian architecture and seasonal flowers.

it is afrikan that woman and man join in smile,
   tears, future.
it is traditional that men and women share
   expectations,
celebrations, struggles.
it is legend that nations start in the family.
it is afrikan that our circle expands.
it is wise that we believe in tomorrows, children,
   quality.
it is written that our vision will equal the
   promise.

so that your nation will live and tell your stories
   accurately,
you must be endless in your loving touch of each
   other.

your unification is the message.
continuance is the answer.

"A Golden Wedding Poem" was written by Rev. L. Burleigh for the fiftieth anniversary celebration of a 19th-century couple, Thomas and Annette Lathrop. They were married in the antebellum period on November 25, 1830, and had ten children.

Thomas and Annette, so you were when young,
And love's song, each to other, fondly sung;
A mutual friends asks if my hands will bring
A friendly tribute as an offering,
To show the honor which my heart would give
To friends so dear, permitted still to live
In sweet accord, in bonds of married life
For fifty swift years, husband and wife.
My willing heart responded, "Yes," at once.
I'll do them honor, gladly for the nonce,
Nor this alone, but every when and where,
I'd multiply their honors here or there!
Some meet reward for dark and shameful days,
Which God has shortened, endless be His praise!
When slavery's ban upon our nation prest,
And negro-hate upreared its dragon crest,
And doddered Taney could no right detect
In colored men, which white ones should respect.

Those days of scorn and hate you knew full well,
And of them still with mixed emotions tell;
Your sorrows rise that men could be so base,
Your joy dilates that better fill their place.
You mourn, perchance, that Hate with her
  garrote
In all the south will let no freedman vote,

If Ku Klux Klans can safely cut his throat;
But you rejoice that Kansas opens wide
Her generous doors to take the swelling tide
Of "Exodus" from wrong and treason doubly
    dyed,
While the south "solid" crowds the north together
To stand united for firm answer, whether
The traitor rebels of that conquered realm
Shall dictate terms to us, or hold the nation's
    helm,
Or yield submissive to what's just and true,
And let the freedmen vote, as we let you.

Through storm or calm your vessel has swept on;
Bravely and well your life work has been done,
Till now, you wait the setting of life's sun.
Five full decades have quickly passed away
Since lapsing Autumn hailed your wedding day.
You cared not then that Summer days were fled,
And frost rime the landscape overspread.
Your hearts were warm and could defy the frost,
Not all caloric have they, as yet, lost;
For true love, married, seldom will grow cold,
Though step and feature tell we're growing old.
Love's flame still burns, with soft and mellow
    light,
And far from fading, groweth yet more bright.
It is a marvel in these divorce days
Of transient unions, matrimonial stays,
That Thomas and Annette should stick together
For fifty years, in every sort of weather.

Letter by Edna Vaughn

Dear Earnest:

Had I known in 1946, having taken my wedding vows, that 50 years later I would be as happy, content as much in love, now more than then, I'd have leaped for joy.

Too old now to leap, I thank God every day for the blessing.

To be still in love, to yet hold hands, to caress and care to be companions in every sense of the word. To do most things together and love it. To be imperfect as is all mankind, yet to allow our imperfections to strengthen us, praise God.

God did not spare us hard times, but praise God, he kept us through them. Remembering the good and the bad, the easy and the difficult times, remembering the rearing of our children. To now behold our 26 grandchildren, 6 great-grandchildren, and our precious children-in-laws and their families is an unexplainable blessing.

To have lived in our home, which we bought when it was built 50 years ago, our children never having had to move—what a blessing—what a joy. How you've kept our home in mint condition. Thank God.

Through my many, many illnesses—you've been right by my side, loving and caring for me, our children, our home.

We have loved each other more than we have loved ourselves. We have kept the romance in our marriage, praise God. Touching, holding, kissing, exchanging terms of tenderness, has been and shall always be so very important, so very necessary.

We've loved when we were lovable and when we were not lovable, through hurt, anger, whatever. We kept on, and keep on loving—not because of but in spite of.

Oh it wasn't hard, was it? When there is true love, loving each other is easy; not a task. So yes, we love each other more than we love ourselves.

It hasn't been the vows that we make. It's been the true, God-ordained love in our hearts for each other that God has blessed us with.

To God be the glory.

—The Gal you married 50 years ago

Apologize

The making up is worth the hurt.
I've not always been lovable and no neither have
*   you,*
But in the midst of all our wrongs we held on,
*   just we two,*
We held on to each other, we held on for dear life.
You've loved me much more than yourself;
I loved you more than mine.
When I was not as I should be, you loved me just
*   the same.*
Most times we didn't give a thought to which one
*   was the blame;*
We held on to each other until all the hurt was
*   gone,*
And we remembered it no more, not a single one.

Tips to a Happy Marriage

Make time for one another.
Treat one another with respect.
It's the little things that count.
Learn to trust.

Be willing to share.
Agree to disagree.
Be willing to give in.
Communicate with one another.
Be affectionate.
Share spiritual growth.
Be kind and considerate to one another.
Be easygoing.
Be flexible about growth and change.
Don't cross the line.
Don't let the sun go down on your wrath.

Although written in 1933, this tale by Chester Himes demonstrates that couples have the same wants and needs throughout time.

A Modern Marriage *

She sucked smoke into her lungs in greedy puffs and let a blue-gray haze dribble slowly through her mouth and nostrils. She crushed the butt out in the tin top of a grease paint jar and glanced at her reflection in the mirror.

She saw a small heart-shaped face, smeared with cosmetics that couldn't hide the beautiful golden bronze of her complexion, a neat head crowned with dark curls perched on a slim body with slim ankles and long legs. Babyish brown eyes that hinted of a blasé sophistication in their babyishness stared back at her. She might have been distinctive if she hadn't been so pretty. The back stage dressing room of the Pythian theater was crowded with brownskin girls who could have passed for her twin.

---

*From *Collected Stories of Chester Himes* by Chester Himes (New York: Thunder's Mouth Press, 1990).

An attendant laid a long white box of flowers on the cluttered dressing table behind her. She picked it up carelessly and slipped the green ribbon, exposing a corsage with white orchids in the dull green tissue paper.

A small, gray gilt-edge card fell to the table top. She glanced casually at the scrawled lines: To a very pretty woman from an admiring man. We will dine at the tea room? and dance at the Crystal Slipper? No name was signed. It was intriguing, she had to admit. He would wait for her at the stage entrance, she mused.

A few names presented themselves to her mind. Ronny, George, Dr. Deserles—all friends of the family. Orchids? She expelled them from her thoughts. The unknown!

A flicker of excitement erased the indifference from her eyes. It was the beckoning of the will-o'-the-wisp of adventure and she responded, however not without a twinge of conscience. That, perhaps, was a lingering, hard-dying trace of a once consuming love of her handsome, fickle, nighthawk husband, Eddie. But thoughts of an empty apartment waiting for her, and a husband who would probably show up late in the morning for aid and not for love, decided her.

She slipped the scant costume from her body and donned an evening gown of jade green, low-necked and no-backed, with tiny Cinderella slippers to match; then re-painted her lips and re-rouged her cheeks, slipped on an imitation Ermine wrap and a little round hat that wasn't quite a derby perched on her midnight curls. She probably would have been a little more attractive with a little less paint.

And had she been a thinking girl, she might have wondered why the unknown man had selected her from all the other chorus girls for the recipient of his favors. But she never taxed her mind with mere causes, she was more interested in results. He had called her a very pretty woman, and had sent her orchids. That was sufficient. She purposely thought of Eddie being out with some other woman, to still the annoying tongue of conscience.

He stood at the stage exit, this young man, tall, handsome, with a cape draped carelessly over his immaculate dress suit. She stepped from the doorway, approached him —and stopped, dead still, shocked into immobility. He bowed with his silk topper to his heart. Tiny ringlets of shining brown curls tumbled over his lean, tan forehead. She stifled an impulse to push those little ringlets back into place.

"You received my flowers?" he questioned.

She regained some of her composure. "Yes, Sir Galahad, but I'm a little disappointed in your eyes," she lisped in a babyish soprano.

He covered his head and straightened. His wide humorous grin was dazzling and his brown eyes twinkled. "But the admiration lies here," he defended himself, lightly touching his heart.

They walked to the brilliantly lighted avenue and he hailed a taxi. It was snowing lightly. The cabbie sighted them and pulled past three fares. She was oddly pleased.

He told her in the cab that his name was Jimmy Guess. She laughed.

"And yours?" he asked.

"Just call me Constance," she replied, and after a pause, "Jimmy."

He offered her a cigarette and held the light. She sank back in her corner and puffed leisurely.

After a while, she said, "I think you're crazy, but I like you just the same." She sounded like she meant it.

He smiled indulgently. "I am crazy," he confessed. "Crazy about you."

The cab put them down in front of the tea room, but they had changed their minds. They continued on to a smoky, noisy night club called the Pirate's Hole.

She found the admiring stares of the men quite flattering as she followed Jimmy to a table, but the sly envious glances of the women were verily honey and nectar. She was strangely proud of her escort. The head waiter was obsequious. He gave them the best table, and gave the station captain the double-price wink.

The music was muted and the lights dim. The champagne warmed their blood. His voice became very tender and he held her closer when they danced. She was gay and responsive and her eyes shone with the kick she was getting out of it.

The orchestra began a low melody interwoven with the beat of African tomtoms. The tempo of the music increased. The rhythm stirred her blood, ate into her self-control like acid. She felt the hot, savage caress of the jungle.

He leaned across the table and turned his gaze from under lowered lids. She saw the hint of urgent demand in his eyes, the smoking passion, felt the shock of her responding passion. She was caught in a mesh of enchantment.

She leaned across the table and touched his arm with her free hand. He looked up. His eyes were questioning.

She said, "Let go," thickly.

He nodded.

They went to an apartment out on Long Street. The ride was hazy to her. She was vaguely irresistible and ineffably sweet.

She groped for his hand and clung to it. He gave her a reassuring pressure and laughed softly. She became conscious of the warm, hard palm of Jimmy's hand. The warmth of his arms about her, his lips brushing her face.

She was passion drunk. He took her arm and led her up the stairs like a child.

They entered the garish parlor. He flung his hat with skilled precision over a statuette on the mantel and took her in his arms. She felt enveloped with a wave of flame. His kisses were brutal, glorious.

She felt herself sinking with a mad, swift plunge below waters of a fathomless sea, drenched with an unspeakable sense of satisfaction. His imitation diamond studs bit into the flesh of her bosom. But she didn't feel them. She received the impression of enraptured bliss.

He opened the bedroom door. She entered. He followed. The door closed behind them.

Her excited, laughing voice came faintly through the panels: "Oh, Eddie, what a lark. I'm so happy. You do love me, don't you?"

Then his voice came muffled: "Sure."

Glossary

Adinkra—A highly valued hand-painted fabric made in Ghana and the Ivory Coast. Created from stamps made of gourd, each representational pattern has a name and offers a proverb or other words of wisdom.

Afoshe—A tasting ceremony.

Afrocentric—A term developed by Molefi Kete Asante for the philosophy that places emphasis on Africa as the source of African-American values, culture, and history. It is synonymous with the term *African-centered*.

Agoo—Give me your attention.

Akan—A clan of people from Ghana who are expert weavers, known for their skill in making *adinkra* and *kente* cloth.

Ameh—You have our attention.

Amen—As God wills it.

Ashe—The power and grace of life for God; equivalent to *amen*.

Asoke—A luxurious embroidered cotton fabric from Nigeria woven by the Yoruba.

Babalawo—Title for a Yoruba priest.

Banns—A wedding announcement made in a church.

Boubou—A type of dress for women, often two-piece and with a full silhouette.

Broom jumping—A cultural marriage tradition where the bride and groom step over a broom to symbolize their new life of matrimony.

Ebo—Offering to Osun.

Harambee—A call to unity: let us pull together.

Irukere—A horsetail broom.

Jocolo—Beaded apron worn by married Ndebele women. Usually made by a mother-in-law for a daughter-in-law.

Karamu—The feast.

Kola nut—An essential ingredient typically used for divination and hospitality. He who brings the kola nut brings life.

Kalimba—An African percussion instrument, also called a thumb piano.

Kente—A cloth with named designs, woven in colorful long strips of cotton or silk and sewn together. Traditionally worn only by royalty, today it is worn for celebrations.

Ketubah—A traditional Jewish wedding contract.

Kufi—A small brimless cap worn by men in Africa.

Kwanzaa—An African-American holiday celebrated from December 26 to January 1.

Libation—A ritual that honors ancestors by pouring a liquid on hallowed ground.

Lobola—Bride price.

Nguzo Saba—The seven guiding principles of Kwanzaa: *umoja*—unity; *kujichagulia*—self-determination; *ujima*—collective responsibility; *ujamaa*—cooperative economics; *nia*—purpose; *kuumba*—creativity; and *imani*—faith.

Obatala—Orisha of creation.

Orishas—Ancestral spirits in Yoruba tradition.

Osun—The Yoruba deity governing love and marriage.

Queh-queh—Pre-wedding celebration held by people of Guyanese descent.

Sankofa—An African word that means to return to the source, "go back and fetch it."

Sorrel—An herb used to make tea or sweet drinks.

Symbols of life—Africans make extensive of use of symbolism throughout their rituals and culture. Wedding services use a tasting of the spices, which can include honey or sugar cane, symbolizing sweetness of marriage; water, used in libation; palm oil, a staple in Nigerian cooking and a symbol of smoothing troubles; kola nut, a essential spice signifying hospitality; wheat, symbolic of fertility; salt, an essential ingredient of life; pepper, symbolizing reconciliation; and bitter herbs, for the growing pains of marriage. In the United States, symbols include a hoe, representing self-sufficiency; a broom, symbolizing cleanliness; and a spear, defense of the home.

Tambiko—A *libation*.

Unity cup—A cup filled with wine or other liquid, used at a wedding ceremony to be shared by the bride and groom and their families.

Yoruba—A clan of people from Nigeria; also the religion of these people.

Atado, Rev. Joe Chuks. *African Marriage Customs and Church Law: A Case-Study of the Igbos.* Kano, Nigeria: Modern Printers, 1988.

Bafoe-Bonnie, Eugene. *Traditional Marriages the African Style.* Langhorne, Pa.: Sankofa Creations, 1993.

Botkin, B. A. *A Treasury of Southern Folklore.* New York: Random House Value Publishing, 1988.

Cole, Harriet. *Jumping the Broom.* New York: Henry Holt & Co., 1993.

Genovese, Eugene. *Roll Jordan Roll.* New York: Vintage Books, 1976.

Green, Danita Rountree. *Broom Jumping: A Celebration of Love.* Richmond, Va.: Entertaining Ideas, Ltd., 1992.

Gutman, Herbert G. *The Black Family in Slavery and Freedom: 1750–1925.* New York: Pantheon Books, 1976.

Le Guennec-Coppens, Françoise. *Wedding Customs in Lamu.* Nairobi: Lamu Society, 1980.

Mbiti, John S. *African Religions and Philosophy.* New York: Anchor Books, 1970.

———. *Introduction to African Religion.* Oxford: Heinemann International, 1991.

———. *Prayers of African Religion.* London: SPCK, 1975; New York: Orbis, 1976.

Middleton, John. The World of the Swahili: An African Mercantile Civilization. New Haven: Yale University Press, 1992.

Neimark, Philip John. *The Way of the Orisa: Empowering Your Life Through the Ancient African Religion of Ifa.* San Francisco: HarperSanFrancisco, 1993.

Nukunya, G. K. *Kinship and Marriage Among the Anlo Ewe.* New York: Humanities Press, 1969.

Starobin, Robert S., ed. *Blacks in Bondage: Letters of American Slaves.* Princeton, N.J.: Wiener, Markus Publishers Inc., 1988.

Wilson, Rev. Willie F. *The African-American Wedding Manual.* Washington, D.C.: House of Knowledge Publishing Co., 1994.

Catering

Ayende—catering, reception. 14 North Market, Philadelphia, PA 19139. 215-222-3522

Isn't That Special Outrageous Cakes—wedding cakes. 147 W. 40 St., New York, NY 10018. 212-722-0678. 720 Monroe St., Hoboken, NJ 07030. 201-216-0123

Priority Wedding Services—bridal consultant, wedding receptions, bridal registry, music. 233 W. Market St., Newark, NJ 07101. 201-242-8012

Spoonbread Inc.—caterers. 333 East 75th St., New York, NY 10021.

Clergy

Rabbi Capers C. Funnye Jr., 10519 S. Church St., Chicago, IL 60643. 312-881-3622

Rev. Emmanuel F. Y. Grantson. Christ Ascension Lutheran Church, 8300 Germantown Ave., Philadelphia, PA 19118. 215-247-4233

Rev. Edward Hunt. Bethel Missionary Baptist Church, 19 South Ave., Wappingers Falls, NY 12590. 914-297-6188

Dr. Osun Dara Nefertiti—ancestral spiritual adviser. 17567 Monica, Detroit, MI 48221. 313-863-5628

Babalawo Ade Ifaleri Olayinka—licensed Yoruba priest. 400 Marion St., Brooklyn, NY 11233. 718-455-0102

Rev. DeForest B. Soaries. First Baptist Church of Lincoln Gardens, 771 Somerset St., Somerset, NJ 08873. 908-828-2009

Rev. Larry Williams. First Baptist Church of Lincoln Gardens, 771 Somerset St., Somerset, NJ 08873. 908-828-2009

Rev. Willie Wilson. Union Temple Baptist Church, 1225 W. St. SE, Washington, D.C. 20020. 202-678-8822, fax: 202-678-6309.

Decorations

Imperial Broom Co.—ceremonial brooms. 214 N. 21st St., Richmond, VA 23223. 804-648-7840

Entertainment

Hallelujah Singers—broom-jumping ceremony, entertainment. 803-525-6129

Montego Joe—master drummer. 55 W. 184th St., Bronx, NY 10468. 718-933-1989 or 212-645-0335

Fashion

Nigerian Fabrics and Fashions—African wedding attire for men and women, wedding consultant. 701 Fulton St., Brooklyn, NY 11217. 800-ADEWUM6 or 718-230-8060

Nu-Heaven's Brides Inc.—wedding attire. 1375 Broadway, 3rd Floor, New York, NY 10018. 212-354-6928, fax: 212-730-6348

Shrine of the Black Madonna Bookstore and Culture Center—African wedding attire, gifts, books, registry. 700 Seward, Detroit, MI 48238. 313-491-0777

Florists

Blooming Elegance—floral arrangements. 2402 Sugar Maple Court, Monmouth Junction, NJ 08852. 908-297-1551 or 800-297-1696

Flowers by Barbara—floral arrangements. 31 Courtlandt St., New Brunswick, NJ 08901. 908-846-0444

Furnishings

African Home—African home furnishings. 297 Decatur St., Brooklyn, NY 11233. 718-363-1159

Afriland—furniture and home furnishings. 501 7th Ave., New York, NY 10018. 212-869-7676

Galerie Hamid—African art, decorations. 41 North 2nd St., Philadelphia, PA 19106. 215-238-9033

Gifts

Ebony Treasures—gifts, black collectibles. P.O. Box 646, Brentwood, NY 11717-2826. Phone/fax: 516-231-4284

Lively Baskets—gifts. P.O. Box 343, Plainsboro, NJ 08536

Panache Ethnic Collectibles & Fine Art—invitations, gifts. Park Plaza 4313, Route 130, Edgewater Park, NJ 08010. 609-835-4111

Progressive Unlimited—handcrafted afrocentric gifts, books, fashions. 14 E. 125th St., New York, NY 10035. 212-427-7084 or 212-724-1110, ext. 1024

Greeting Cards, Invitations

Carol Joy Creations—greeting cards. 26 Mill Plain Rd., Danbury CT 06811. 203-798-2060, fax: 203-748-5315

Kuumba Collectibles—greeting cards, gifts. P.O. Box 91163, Washington, D.C. 20090-1163. 202-797-8823

Unique Invitations. 147 W. 40th St., New York, NY 10018. 212-722-0678 and 720 Monroe St., Hoboken, NJ 07030. 201-216-0123

Wedding Consultants

African American Brides of Distinction—wedding consultants, African-American bridal shows. 510-832-0303

The Kearns Group—bridal consultant, events planner. 9140 E. Prairie Rd., Evanston, IL 60203. 847-673-6310

OMB Services—specialty African weddings. 1202 Village Lane, Winter Park, FL 32792. Phone/fax 407-657-1194

Lois Pearce—bridal consultant. P.O. Box 5636, Hamden, CT 06518. 203-248-2661

Saala Enterprises—Saala Shabazz, wedding planner. P.O. Box 76122, Los Angeles, CA 90076. 213-957-4900

Shirley Spruill—wedding planner. Touch of Elegance Black Bridal Showcase. 9 Vince Rd., Somerset, NJ 08873. 908-846-1380

Yaffa Productions—wedding consultants, dancers, drummers, entertainment. Linda Humes, 122 W. 17th St., New York, NY 10011. 212-840-1234

Wedding Sites and Receptions

Akwaaba Mansion. 347 MacDonough St., Brooklyn, NY 11233. 718-455-5958

National Black Theater—wedding sanctuary, caterers, wedding planning. Harlem, New York, NY. 212-722-3800

Other

African Wedding Guide—guide to planning an African-centered wedding. http://www.mela-net.com/melanet/wedding/wed.html

Leslyn Johnson, Toucan Communications Inc.—video production company. 10906 Kencrest Dr., Mitchellville, MD 20721. 301-464-5585

Shrine of Ptah and Temple Nebt-Het—fasting, cleansing, purification rituals. 106 Kingston Ave., Brooklyn, NY 11213. 718-221-HEAL

Signature Bride—bridal magazine. 101 Grand Ave., Chicago, IL 60610. 312-527-6590, fax: 312-527-6596

Twin Oaks Inn—bed and breakfast. P.O. Box 1767, Vineyard Haven, MA 02568. 800-696-8633, 508-693-8633, fax: 508-693-5833

Index